The Great Book of Badass Women

15 Fearless and Inspirational Women that Changed History

Rachel Walsh and Bill O'Neill

ISBN-13: 978-1-64845-066-2

DON'T FORGET YOUR FREE BOOKS

CONTENTS

INTRODUCTION

There have been countless badass women who have changed the world for the better, yet most people have never even heard of them. Women throughout history have fought for their rights and the rights of others, defended their countries during wartime, healed the sick and the wounded, invented new technologies, led countries, made inspiring art, and so much more.

This collection of biographies and quick trivia facts aims to tell the stories of the courageous and tenacious women who have paved the way for the women of the future. It's difficult to choose just 15 badass women; however, these particular ladies fearlessly broke society's norms and weren't afraid to stand out. They were extraordinary and often way ahead of their time.

In the 18th and 19th centuries, many women took a passive role in society because that's what men dictated to them. Most women during this period remained primarily in the domestic sphere, and the men who surrounded them treated them as property. But some women refused to be passive, even though that's what society demanded of them, and took control of their freedom.

Ching Shih, a 16-year-old Chinese teenager, went from a sex worker in a brothel to the commander of a fleet of 70,000 pirates. Sojourner Truth took her infant daughter and escaped to freedom with little more than a handkerchief of food on her back. Florence Nightingale lay the foundation for women to serve in vocations outside the home by founding the modern field of nursing.

The 20th century was a critical time for women. Many women around the world finally got the right to vote, were admitted to colleges previously exclusive to male students, or began to be recognized for their scientific achievements, their athletic abilities, and their art.

Alice Paul and the National Woman's Party put their lives on the line to fight for women's suffrage in the United States. They picketed the White House during wartime, were thrown in jail, and endured brutal treatment for the right to vote.

After the hard-fought battles for women's rights in the 20th century, many think that the 21st century is a time when women don't have to fight any longer for their most basic rights, like the freedom for girls and women to get an education. Yet, in 2012, a 15-year-old girl living in Pakistan, Malala Yousafzai, was shot in the head by the Taliban after advocating for girls' right to education.

In the United States, women's reproductive rights are still under attack, hanging on by a thread with little more to keep them than the dedication and courage of 87-year-old Supreme Court Justice Ruth Bader Ginsburg. So, the fight taken up by women in the 20th century has been handed down to today's women and girls, who continue their struggle.

There have been so many badass women in history, that it was nearly impossible to choose only 15. Women have been badass because they have to be, and they'll continue to fight for their rights until they have them. These are just a few of those heroes, but many women are heroes every day, and we will probably never know most of their names.

CHAPTER 1:

CHING SHIH

Typically, when one reads about pirates or sees them in the movies, they are depicted as men. However, there were numerous fearless female pirates, and Ching Shih was the most badass of them all. Although she is not well-known, many historians argue that Ching Shih was the most successful pirate in history.

Historians know little about the early life of Ching Shih, the Pirate Queen. While no one knows her actual birthday, her estimated birth year is 1775, and she was born in the city of Guangzhou, the capital of the province of Guangdong, China. She was born Shih Yang, and later became known as Cheng I Sao, which translates to *"wife of Cheng."* The name by which she is commonly referred to in history is Ching Shih, which means *"Widow Ching."*

Rumored to be quite beautiful, Ching Shih spent her teenage years working in a floating brothel in Canton, China. Floating brothels were quite common at the time and were known as *"flower boats."* The boats would sail along the coast and pick up paying customers along the way. Ching Shih used her position as a sex worker to learn secrets about the rich and powerful and use them to her advantage.

At the young age of 16, Ching Shih married her first husband, Zheng Yi, a feared pirate who came from a long line of notorious pirates, dating back to the mid-17th century. Zheng Yi became attracted to Ching Shih's beauty and knew right away that he wanted to marry her. There are numerous stories about how they came to be married. Some say that he proposed, while other accounts claim that he ordered his pirates to pillage the floating brothel and capture Ching Shih.

Ching Shih was already a smart businesswoman and negotiated the best possible deal for herself in her new marriage. Ching Shih's marriage stipulations argued for true equality and nothing less. She requested the rights to half of her husband's proceeds, which included all the *"booty"* he took, as well as equality in decision making.

The money wasn't enough; she understood that power was just as important if she was going to have control over her destiny. Ching Shih was far ahead of her time; marriage equality was far from the norm in China in 1801.

Before he married Ching Shih, Zheng Yi was already a powerful pirate, commanding an entire fleet of around 200 pirate ships known as the "Red Flag Fleet." With Ching Shih's help, the dynamic pirate duo grew their fleet to include roughly 1,200 ships and an estimated 50,000 to 70,000 crew members at any given time.

They ruled the Chinese seas, and the Chinese government knew it. In 1804, the Zhengs decided to not only assert their power over the Chinese rulers but the colonial powers as well. They blockaded the Portuguese trading port, which was located in Macau at the time. Portugal attempted to defend its port but was defeated by the powerful pirate couple.

After only six short years of marriage, Zheng Yi died in a hurricane in Vietnam aged just 39. Following her husband's death, Ching Shih was not about to walk away as a powerless widow. After her husband's death, some of the fleet captains tried to run away. In a swift action to solidify her rule, she gave the ship captains two options: they could attempt escape, and probably die, or they could serve under a woman. She also cleverly surrounded herself with allies and troops to back her up. She swiftly got command of the fleet, and the pirates learned to report to a woman.

As a woman pirate in charge, Ching Shih had strict rules and ran a tight ship. The punishments for those who broke the rules were severe. Stealing from villagers or the communal pirate treasury was punishable by death. Those who deserted or committed other acts of disobedience lost their heads. Those who committed less severe crimes lost their ears instead of their head.

Ching Shih also developed strict policies regarding the treatment of women, and those who abused or raped women were not treated kindly under her watch. Life as a pirate involved taking prisoners; that was just part of the trade. However, Ching Shih decreed that, if the prisoners were women, there were strict procedures that had to be followed.

Women deemed ugly were to be released unharmed. Beautiful women had a different fate; there was a possibility that they could be given to their captors as a wife. But, if the crew member wanted to marry the woman, they had to be faithful and vow to take care of her. Abusing women was not permitted, and sex that wasn't consensual was punishable by death. Men who raped women lost their heads, and adultery was also punishable by death.

Despite her harsh rules, Ching Shih commanded a well-oiled machine after the death of her husband, and her power grew. She was the ruler of the seas from Macau to Canton. Her Red Flag Fleet plundered coastal towns and villages and recruited more men to join their ranks along the way. The pirates even demanded that Chinese citizens pay them taxes. She became such a threat to the Emperor of China that he eventually ordered a fleet of ships to attack Ching Shih and her fleet.

Ching Shih and her crew defeated the ships sent to destroy her, capturing 60 ships and their crew members in the process. She gave the captured crew members two options: be nailed to the deck of their ship or work for Ching Shih. Most men chose the second option.

The Chinese government eventually turned to the British for help to defeat Ching Shih, but not even the British superpower could take down the great Ching Shih. The British lent the Chinese a warship, the HMS *Mercury*, which was joined by Portuguese ships, but Ching Shih and her crew evaded them all.

Things finally came to a head for badass Ching Shih and her pirate crew in 1809 with the Battle of Tiger's Mouth. The British, Portuguese, and Chinese decided to join forces to defeat Ching Shih. Stories vary here; some say that Ching Shih requested amnesty from the Chinese government, while other sources say that the Chinese government offered her the deal.

Regardless, Ching Shih was not about to go down without a good negotiation. She demanded stipulations for her surrender that not only benefited herself, but also her crew. By the time she completed her talks, she had arranged to keep all of her money, 80 junks (traditional Chinese sailing ships) for her personal use, and 40 additional ships for trading salt.

Ching Shih didn't forget to advocate for her crew. For her team, she negotiated a policy whereby, when her pirate confederation ceased to exist, her crew could give up their life of piracy and get a position in the Chinese empire instead.

Out of the 17,318 pirates under her command, 60 pirates were banished, 151 were exiled, and 126 were put to death. All of the remaining pirates in her crew surrendered their weapons and gave up their pirating ways.

In her retirement from the badass pirate life, Ching Shih used the money she had made to become a retired badass. She opened a gambling house and a brothel. She also dabbled in the salt trade and continued making money.

After an amazing and adventurous life, Ching Shih died in 1844 at the age of 69. She died peacefully, surrounded by her family.

CHING SHIH: DID YOU KNOW?

1. After her husband died, Ching Shih took his adopted son, Cheung Po Tsai, as her lover. Cheung Po joined the pirate fleet after being captured as a teenager. He slowly ascended the ranks, eventually being raised as part of the Zheng family. Cheung Po was only 21 at the time of his adoptive father's death, but he and Ching Shih had a sexual relationship, and later married. Cheung Po served as second-in-command in all the major battles in which Ching Shih fought.

2. Mistress Ching from *Pirates of the Caribbean: At World's End* was inspired by Ching Shih. Actress Takayo Fischer plays Ching Shih.

3. In 1809, Ching Shih captured Richard Glasspoole, a British officer of the East India Company, as well as seven sailors. They were kept as prisoners for over three months.

4. Ching Shih and Zheng Yi had two sons during their short time together. The boys' names were Cheng Ying Shi and Cheng Heung Shi, but little is known about them.

5. Famous actress Maggie Shiu starred in the Hong Kong series *Captain of Destiny* as a character based on Ching Shih.

6. Ching Shih and Cheung Po Tsai were married for 10 years and had two children together, a son and a daughter.

7. Ching Shih became a military advisor to the Chinese army leader Lin Zexu during the First Opium War.

8. Madam Ching was so badass that when the Chinese government released so-called *"suicide ships"* filled with explosives to destroy her fleet, she evaded them, so they exploded without damage to her fleet. She then took control of the exploded *"suicide ships"* and repaired them to use in her fleet.

9. A graphic novel, *Afterlife,* was inspired by Ching Shih. In the book, Ching Shih is a mighty female warrior who battles demons in the afterlife.

10. Cheung Po Tsai Cave, named after Ching Shih's second husband, is located in Hong Kong. According to legend, Cheung Po Tsai hid his pirate's treasure in the cave.

CHAPTER 2:

FLORENCE NIGHTINGALE

Badass women defy the social norms of their time and pursue their dreams against all odds. Florence Nightingale followed her calling to be a nurse, during a time when nursing wasn't an established or respected field for women, particularly women of a higher class. Despite the controversy, Nightingale became the founder of modern nursing.

Florence Nightingale was born in 1820 in Florence, Italy, while her wealthy English family was traveling abroad. She was named after her birth city, as was her sister (Parthenope). Florence received an excellent education, unlike many young women of her time. She was schooled at home by her father and developed a love of learning early on in life. In addition to her love of learning, she also found joy in helping others.

When Florence was just a young girl, she could be found traveling to the village with her mother, carrying medicine and much needed supplies to sick neighbors who were living in poverty.

By the time she was a teenager, Florence had already decided that being a nurse was her divine purpose. Her parents not only disapproved of her career aspirations; they forbade them. They saw nursing as a dirty profession, reserved for lower-class drunkards. There was little in the way of professional training for nursing at the time, and it wasn't a common profession for women from middle- and upper-class families.

Florence's parents wanted her to marry a nice man and disapproved of her attending any type of nursing school. When she was just 17 years old, Florence had already started refusing marriage proposals. She refused to marry a man named Richard Monckton Milnes, who her parents saw as a suitable marriage prospect.

In an attempt to distract her from her nursing passion, Florence's parents decided to send her traveling around Europe. Despite this, Florence continued studying on her own during her travels. She also met an acquaintance, Sidney Herbert, who later played a part in her kick-starting her nursing career.

After returning home to England and continuing to make it clear that she had no interest in marriage, Florence's parents finally succumbed and sent her to a nursing school in Germany. She attended Pastor Theodore Fliedner's hospital and school for Lutheran Deaconesses for three months. While there, she had a variety of helpful experiences, from bathing patients to observing surgeries. Following her training in Germany, she traveled to Paris for additional schooling with the Sisters of Mercy.

Nightingale returned to England after getting her education and began managing a hospital in London. In 1854, Nightingale received word of the harsh conditions being suffered by the soldiers in the Crimean War, from Sidney Herbert, the Secretary of War.

She decided to go to the war front to care for wounded soldiers. Herbert appointed her to lead a group of nurses in the hospital at Scutari, in modern-day Istanbul, Turkey. This was where Florence Nightingale became world-renowned for her nursing efforts.

In her newly appointed post as the Superintendent of the Female Nurses in the Hospitals in the East, Nightingale's first order of business was finding other qualified nurses to accompany her to the front. She got to work interviewing nurses who were up for the job, but few seemed like they would be competent enough based on Nightingale's standards.

After interviewing hundreds of women, she ultimately chose only 38, many of them nuns, to accompany her to Turkey. After a long, arduous journey by sea, during which

Nightingale was extremely ill, they arrived at the hospital in Turkey, and faced circumstances beyond anything they could have imagined.

The conditions were beyond unsanitary; sick and wounded men were sleeping in their filth, there were rats and fleas, and bloody rags littered the floor. The nurses' first task was to improve the cleanliness of the hospital. They mopped and scrubbed, changed sheets, repaired bedding, changed bandages, and removed the bloody rags that were haphazardly strewn about the hospital.

Despite the doctors' initial reservations about the women being part of a war zone, they soon began to notice that the patients were getting better. The improved cleanliness of the hospital made a huge difference in the health of the patients.

Nightingale grasped early on that there was a clear and immediate link between unsanitary conditions and high mortality rates. In February 1855, 42.7% of patients died in the hospital. By June, after Nightingale and her nurses had implemented more sanitary conditions, the mortality rate had gone down to 2%.

Nightingale and her team of nurses went beyond improving the sanitary conditions of the hospital. They implemented something that Nightingale called the *"invalid's kitchen,"* where they prepared special food for patients with dietary restrictions.

They also started a laundry service, so there would always be clean linens and clothing. Nightingale even thought about intellectual activities for the patients and created a classroom and library. She left no stone unturned in her revolutionary work in nursing during the war.

During this time, Nightingale also gained a reputation for genuinely caring about her patients, earning her the popular nickname, *"Lady of the Lamp."* She would often go from bed to bed with her lamp, checking on her patients, long after all the other nurses had gone to bed. Poet Henry Wadsworth Longfellow immortalized this image of Nightingale with his poem, *"Santa Filomena."*

When Nightingale returned from the Crimean War, after spending about a year and a half in Turkey, she came home a hero, although she didn't seem to care for the attention or fame. She received a prize of £250,000 for her efforts from the British government, which she used to do even more for the field of nursing.

Nightingale used her money to found St. Thomas' Hospital, where she created the Nightingale Training School for Nurses. With nursing no longer seen as an undesirable profession, thanks to Nightingale, many young women—including women from the upper class—enrolled in the training school. Finally, nurses received the training they needed to make a massive difference in healthcare, not just in England, but around the world.

In addition to founding a school to train nurses, Nightingale returned from the war determined to write down what she had learned. She used statistics to prove that her methods in Turkey worked. Her report, *Notes on Matters Affecting the*

Health, Efficiency and Hospital Administration of the British Army, proposed reforms for military hospitals. Her research from the war resulted in the creation of a Royal Commission for the Health of the Army.

While her report was outstanding, Nightingale is best known for another piece of work she published after her time in Crimea, *Notes on Nursing,* which became a seminal text for modern nursing. It was the first time anything like that had been written and it is still considered a classic introduction to the nursing profession.

Despite everything she accomplished, Nightingale's life was not without its difficulties. Her time in Crimea had taken an extreme toll on her health. She had contracted brucellosis, a bacterial infection also known as Crimean fever. She never fully recovered. By the young age of 38, Nightingale was often bedridden. She remained homebound for the rest of her life.

But being bedridden didn't stop her; she continued working from her bed, writing an estimated 200 books, articles, and pamphlets on nursing throughout her life. Some may wonder when the Lady of the Lamp had time for marriage and family, and the answer is: she didn't. The life she wanted to lead left no time for marriage.

Florence Nightingale was bestowed many honors in her lifetime. Florence received the Order of Merit, which was presented to her by King Edward in 1907. She also became the first woman ever to receive the Freedom of the City of London in 1908.

In 1910, Nightingale became ill and passed away suddenly on August 13, 1910, while at home in London. She was a hero—and she knew it—but she was never a fan of being famous. She just didn't care for all the fanfare. Florence's family was asked if they would allow her to be buried at the famous Westminster Abbey, a place reserved for the most influential people in England.

The request alone is an enormous honor, but her family politely declined. Florence was laid to rest in her family plot at St. Margaret's Church in Hampshire, England, which was her dying wish.

FLORENCE NIGHTINGALE: DID YOU KNOW?

1. Nightingale was fluent in four languages: English, French, German, and Italian. As if that weren't impressive enough, she even had a solid understanding of Latin and classical Greek; however, she wasn't fluent.

2. Nightingale had a unique pet, a baby owl, which she rescued on her travels in Athens, Greece, in 1850. She named the owl Athena and used to carry the bird around in her pocket. Athena passed away when Florence went to serve as a nurse in the Crimean War.

3. Not only did Nightingale never marry, she also turned down numerous marriage proposals, including one proposal by her cousin, Henry Nicholson.

4. As if Nightingale wasn't busy enough founding the entire field of nursing, she also wrote a passionate novel called *Cassandra*. The book was an angry attack on the Victorian family, a clear expression of Nightingale's frustration at the restrictions she faced as an upper-class woman. She addressed the fact that women weren't allowed to rise to their full potential and were restricted from entering professions where they could make a difference in the world. Nightingale denounced the lives of idleness she and other women of her class were forced to lead.

Cassandra later became an essential piece of work for the feminist movement.

5. Queen Victoria thought Nightingale was remarkable. She even went so far as to send her a brooch to say thank you for her services and requested to meet her when she returned to England. The two did end up meeting and stayed in touch over the years.

6. America's *"First trained nurse,"* Linda Richards, was trained by Nightingale when she attended London's Nightingale School of Nursing.

7. Since 1974, Nightingale's birthday, May 12, has been designated International Nurses Day.

8. During the American Civil War, the United States government frequently consulted Nightingale about hospital management and how to improve mortality rates and sanitation.

9. There is a Florence Nightingale Museum, which is located on the original site of the Nightingale Training School for Nurses in London. The museum has more than 2,000 artifacts and commemorates the life of the founder of modern nursing.

10. Ever heard of medical tourism? It's trendy today, but it was born because of Nightingale herself. She traveled all over the world, learning about healthcare and medicine. Nightingale would encourage patients to go to other countries where medical procedures and drugs were cheaper, so they could afford what they needed.

CHAPTER 3:

ALICE PAUL

A badass is someone who fights for what they want, and there have been few people in history who have fought as long and as hard as Alice Paul. She dedicated her entire life to fighting for equal rights for women, often to the detriment of her health and well-being.

Alice Paul was born on January 11, 1885, in Moorestown, New Jersey. Alice came from a wealthy Quaker family, who resided on a 265-acre farm called *Paulsdale*. Despite their wealth, the family lived simply, and Alice learned to work hard at an early age.

Her religious background and heritage served as her initial inspiration toward her commitment to women's rights. In the Quaker community in which she grew up, gender equality was valued and women who were educated and accomplished were admired. Alice Paul's lifelong beliefs in social justice and equality for women were developed early on in her life.

As a child, Alice observed the women in her community completing tasks and activities outside of the home and family. Her mom, Tacie Paul, participated in women's suffrage meetings and Alice sometimes attended the gatherings with her.

Alice was lucky enough to receive an outstanding education, just as good as the males in her family. At age six, she started at Moorestown Friends School, a private Quaker school, and graduated in 1901 when she was just 16. She then went to Swarthmore College outside of Philadelphia, Pennsylvania.

While in college, Paul again defied the norms and pursued studies in science, which was uncommon for women during this time. Paul graduated from Swarthmore in 1905 and moved to the Big Apple, New York City, on her own. She got a job working in a settlement house, one of the few places women could get jobs at that time. Settlement house women lived and worked with people living in poverty and provided services like education, recreational opportunities, and healthcare.

After living in New York City for a year, Paul moved back to Philadelphia to go to graduate school at the prestigious University of Pennsylvania, where she again excelled in her studies. She majored in sociology and had two minors: political science and economics. She finished her degree in a little over a year and then sailed for Europe.

The purpose of Paul's travel was more education. She continued her schooling at Woodbrooke, a Quaker school in England. It was during her time living in England that Alice Paul started to show what a badass she was.

During her time in England, Paul began pursuing women's suffrage work with the Women's Social and Political Union (WSPU), an organization founded in 1903 by Emmeline Pankhurst and her daughters Christabel and Sylvia. The WSPU was militant and much more aggressive than the women's suffrage organizations in the United States at the time. Alice Paul slowly moved up the organization's ranks until she was participating in the most daring of the suffrage protests.

In one particularly gutsy protest, Paul and her fellow suffragette, Amelia Brown, disguised themselves as cleaners so they could sneak into a hall where a banquet was being held for the Mayor of London. One of the women broke a window with their shoe, and they shouted, *"Votes for women!"* while the Prime Minister of the United Kingdom was giving a speech. For their protest, Paul and Brown were sent to jail for a month.

Paul participated in many militant acts in England and got used to being thrown in jail; it happened multiple times. In prison, she staged hunger strikes to gain attention for the suffragist cause. When Paul returned to the United States in 1910, she brought her militant suffragist training with her. Determined to get American women the vote, she became involved in suffrage work right away.

It quickly became clear that her methods didn't fit the mold of the traditional women's suffrage movement in the United States. The National American Woman Suffrage Association (NAWSA) didn't like Paul's bold and militant tactics. Instead of backing down, Paul founded a new suffrage organization called the National Woman's Party. She didn't hold back when it came to fighting for women's suffrage.

The members of the National Woman's Party engaged in numerous daring protests; most infamously, their daily picketing of the White House, which began on January 10, 1917. The protest drew the public's ire and was very controversial. The brave women stood outside from 10:00 am until 5:30 p.m. every day, all year long, in all kinds of weather including sleet, snow, and hail. They announced they would remain at their posts until there was a federal amendment passed granting American women the right to vote.

Even after the United States officially entered World War I, the women decided to continue picketing the White House, even though they were sure they would be arrested. At first, the sentences were short, but as the women continued protesting, the sentences extended, with the longest one lasting seven months.

While imprisoned, Paul was forced to strip naked and wear prison clothing. She wasn't given much food at all. The women were refused essential sanitary items like toilet paper and were supposed to eat all meals in silence. Despite facing these harsh circumstances in jail, Paul continued to fight. Shortly after her longest prison sentence of seven months began, Paul initiated a hunger strike to boycott the horrible treatment of the prisoners and the government's refusal to treat them as political prisoners.

Paul didn't stop at the hunger strike. The women were having trouble breathing in the jail, so Paul demanded that the guards open a window. When they refused, Paul threw a book of the poems of Browning out the window. The guards locked Paul into solitary confinement for the rest of her sentence. While in solitary confinement, she continued to refuse food and was eventually force-fed after officials feared she was near death.

Eventually, the White House administration gave in to public pressure to release the women. Thirty women were on a hunger strike, eight of whom were extremely ill and on the verge of collapse. The White House didn't want to have any deaths on their hands. Shortly after the release of the suffragists, President Woodrow Wilson pledged his support for an amendment to the United States Constitution, granting women the right to vote.

The 19th Amendment to the United States Constitution granting women the right to vote was finally ratified on August 18, 1920. Alice Paul and the National Woman's Party contributed a great deal to this monumental piece of legislation in United States history.

After women won the right to vote, Alice Paul didn't stop and take a breather. She immediately devoted herself to a new cause, working on an Equal Rights Amendment for women. In 1923, Paul introduced the Equal Rights Amendment in the United States Congress, but it did not pass.

Paul also worked on women's rights at an international level. From the 1920s to the 1950s, she traveled throughout South America and Europe. She founded the World Woman's Party (WWP) in 1938, with headquarters in Geneva, Switzerland. The WWP worked with the League of Nations to ensure that equality for women was enshrined in the United Nations Charter. It also played a crucial role in the creation of the United Nations Commission on the Status of Women.

Paul returned to the United States in 1941, after tireless work abroad for women's equality around the world. Once home, she led a coalition that successfully pushed for a sexual discrimination clause in the 1964 Civil Rights Act. She also never gave up on the Equal Rights Amendment.

Unfortunately, Paul didn't live to see the Equal Rights Amendment ratified. In fact, to date, the Equal Rights Amendment has not been passed in the United States. Paul never married and never had children. Her devotion to the causes she believed in was her life. She worked diligently for women's rights until she suffered a stroke and was no longer able to do so. Paul died in Moorestown, NJ, on July 9, 1977. She left behind a legacy, one that demonstrates that one person can make an incredible difference in the world.

ALICE PAUL: DID YOU KNOW?

1. Although it was uncommon during her time, that didn't stop Alice Paul from participating in sports, which she loved. She played baseball, basketball, and even hockey! There is no doubt her incredible physical strength got her through years of protests, hunger strikes, and force-feedings.

2. Paul suffered from 55 force-feedings in prison in London and endured another 25 in jail in the United States in 1917. She suffered from severe digestive issues for years after being force-fed and lost her sense of smell.

3. Modesty was a prominent quality of Paul's. She hated being in the spotlight, even though, as the leader of her suffrage organization, she always was.

4. Paul organized the first women's march, which was a grand parade of women marching up Pennsylvania Avenue. The parade was planned around President Wilson's inauguration on March 13, 1913. Sound familiar?

5. Alice Paul organized a cross-country road trip for women in the National Woman's Party that traveled from San Francisco to Washington, D.C., in 1915. There were no maps, and the transcontinental highway had yet to be completed. Paul sent them on quite the adventure!

6. Eating meat was described by Paul as being *"cannibalistic,"* and she was a vegetarian for most of her life.

7. In 1984, the Alice Paul Institute was founded at Paul's childhood home in Paulsdale, New Jersey. The Institute honors Paul's legacy by educating the public about her critical work and offers heritage and girls' leadership development programs. Paulsdale, home of the Institute, is now a National Historic Landmark.

8. The Equal Rights Amendment was first drafted by Alice Paul herself in 1923.

9. In 1943, the Equal Rights Amendment was rewritten and dubbed the Alice Paul Amendment.

10. There was a popular movie released by HBO in 2004, *Iron Jawed Angels,* which highlights Alice Paul and the National Woman's Party's work in the fight for women's suffrage in the United States. The movie stars Hilary Swank as Alice Paul.

CHAPTER 4:

RUTH BADER GINSBURG

There is no denying the fact that Ruth Bader Ginsburg, also known as the *"Notorious RBG,"* is a rock star and has radically changed the world for women. RBG's generation faced constant sexism, and it wasn't out of the ordinary.

Many women fell in line, got married, stayed home, and cared for their children. Understandably, the pressure of society's expectations impeded their ability to put their natural skills and intellect on show outside the home. But Ginsburg refused to fall in line. The sexism in society was just one more thing she conquered. She continues to fight on behalf of all women, every day of her life.

The Notorious RBG was born Joan Ruth Bader on March 15, 1933, in Brooklyn, New York. Her family—mother Celia, father Nathan, and older sister Marilyn—lived in Flatbush, a low-income working-class neighborhood at the time.

Ruth didn't come from a prestigious family. Her father was a Jewish immigrant from Ukraine, who sold furs and then later became a haberdasher (someone who sells menswear). One of the biggest influences in Ruth's life was her mother, Celia, who instilled in her the importance of education and frequently took her to the library. Celia never had the opportunity to attend college; instead, she worked in a garment factory to pay for her brother's college education.

When Ruth was 14 months old, her family faced tragedy; her sister Marilyn, who was six years old, died of meningitis. Those who know Ruth describe her as a deep thinker, and she was a ravenous learner from an early age. She attended James Madison High School in Brooklyn, where she did exceptionally well. Ruth graduated high school at the young age of 15.

Unfortunately, Ruth's mother struggled with cancer throughout Ruth's high school years and passed away the day before her graduation.

After high school, Ruth went on to earn her bachelor's degree from Cornell University, where she studied government. Again, she excelled in her studies and graduated first in her

31

class. In 1954, the same year that she graduated, she married Martin *"Marty"* D. Ginsburg, a law student.

As newlyweds, they faced many challenges. They had their first baby, a daughter who they named Jane, shortly after Marty was drafted for two years of military service. When he was discharged two years later, the Ginsburgs both enrolled at Harvard Law School.

At Harvard, Ruth Ginsburg was one of nine women in a class of five hundred students in the prestigious law school. Not only did she get in, she also outshone her class. She became the first woman to be a part of the Harvard Law Review, which was extremely competitive. Ginsburg accomplished all of this while caring for Jane.

Later in life, Ginsburg recalled the inherent discrimination that women faced while studying law at Harvard. When she was a young law student, she was invited to a dinner with the dean, along with the eight other women who were in the law program. The dean asked the women why they thought they were worthy enough to take away a place at the school from a man.

Ginsburg was never afraid to speak out regarding Harvard's treatment of women. She has spoken publicly about being shut out of the university's Lamont Library because women were barred from entering. Even though she was a top student and made the Harvard Law Review, women were not invited to the Review banquet.

As if being a full-time law student and taking care of a baby were not enough, Ginsburg then faced another devastating challenge. In 1956, Marty was diagnosed with testicular cancer and required extensive medical treatment. Ginsburg cared for him and their daughter, all while continuing not only her studies, but assisting with her husband's as well. She would get notes from his classmates and copy them down for him.

Marty beat his cancer, recovered, and graduated from Harvard Law School. Shortly after, he got a job at a law firm in New York City. Ginsburg went with him, which meant leaving Harvard, despite her success there. When they arrived in NYC, Ginsburg enrolled at Columbia Law School, where she again excelled and graduated first in her class. However, it turned out that, in the 1950s, graduating first in your class at Columbia wasn't enough to get a job in NYC, simply because of gender. No law firms would hire her.

Ginsburg's career finally started with a clerking position for the U.S. District Judge Edmund L. Palmieri. Then, in 1963, she began teaching at Rutgers University, becoming the second woman ever to teach full time there. She received a *"modest"* salary because her husband already had a well-paid position.

The Notorious RBG was just getting started though. By 1965, she had published her first book, *Civil Procedure in Sweden*, and the same year she had a son, James Ginsburg, born on September 8, 1965. The 1970s is when Ginsburg started to shine in the women's rights arena. In 1972, she co-founded the American Civil Liberties Union (ACLU) Women's Rights

Project and became the first woman ever to become a tenured professor at Columbia Law School.

In the 1970s, Ginsburg spent her time slowly building a case for women's equality in small, incremental steps. Between 1973 and 1975, she argued six gender discrimination cases before the Supreme Court, winning five of them.

Surprisingly, not all of these cases that RBG argued were on behalf of women. RBG had the radical idea that defending men against gender inequality was likely to get her point across. She took on the case of a young male widower who, after the death of his wife, devoted his time to caring for their baby instead of working. When he applied for Social Security benefits that were available to widows, he was denied. When Ruth heard of the case, she immediately agreed to take it on.

In this landmark case, Weinberger v. Wiesenfeld, the young widower had a unanimous victory. This was one of several essential contributions to men and women's equality made by Ginsburg in the Supreme Court. Ginsburg remains friends with Wiesenfeld to this day. Forty years after this iconic case, RBG officiated the wedding of 71-year-old Wiesenfeld and his bride, Elaine Harris. Jason Wiesenfeld, the little boy at the center of the 1975 case, was an attendee of the wedding.

In 1980, Ginsburg was appointed to the U.S. Court of Appeals for the District of Columbia Circuit by President Jimmy Carter. Of course, she didn't stop her continuous ascent there. President Bill Clinton appointed Ginsburg as the second female and the first Jewish female to serve as a Supreme

Court Justice of the United States in 1993. RBG is known for being a cautious judge, who shows moderation and never raises her voice or gets angry. She is renowned for strongly advocating for gender equality, workers' rights, and the separation of church and state.

One of the cases she is most known for presiding over is the landmark 1996 case *United States v. Virginia*. In this infamous case, the Supreme Court ruled that the Virginia Military Institute could not continue to refuse to admit women, as it had been doing. RBG has been a guest speaker at countless events and won many awards. In 1999, she won the American Bar Association's Thurgood Marshall Award for her influential contributions to civil rights and gender equality for all.

Although she never really tries to be funny and does not like small talk, Ginsburg knows how to get a reaction. For example, Ginsburg states, *"When I'm sometimes asked when there will be enough [women on the Supreme Court], and I say, 'When there are nine,' people are shocked. But there'd been nine men, and nobody's ever raised a question about that."* No one better exemplifies the feminist rallying cry, *"Nevertheless, she persisted."* The Notorious RBG fights for women every day; she has earned every ounce of her superhero status.

RUTH BADER GINSBURG: DID YOU KNOW?

1. When she was just a newlywed, Ginsburg took the civil service exam and qualified to be a claims adjuster. After stating that she was three months pregnant with her daughter, her civil service ranking was reduced, along with her pay. She learned early on that women were being discriminated against because of their gender.

2. When Ginsburg was appointed to the Supreme Court, there was no bathroom on site for women. She would have to go back to Sandra Day O'Connor's judge's chambers to use the restroom. Shortly after Ginsburg was appointed, the United States government finally installed a women's restroom. This was in 1993!

3. Ginsburg had a truly equal partnership with her husband, Marty, a rare dynamic. Marty was a great cook and even baked cakes for Ginsburg's clerks' birthdays. He often had to drag Ginsburg home from her office to have a good meal and get some sleep.

4. Ginsburg is known as this Supreme Court's *"great dissenter."*

5. Those who have seen the Notorious RBG in her robes might wonder about the unique collars she always wears. Ginsburg and Sandra Day O'Connor felt that Supreme

Court robes were designed for men, so they agreed to wear jabots as a point of difference. Jabots are a pleated frill of cloth or lace attached to the front of a blouse or dress. The women wanted to stand out in the sea of black. Ginsburg has two signature jabots that she is known for wearing.

6. Ginsburg has a personal trainer and works out diligently, twice a week. She doesn't just walk on a treadmill or do water aerobics like many stereotypical 87-year-olds. She does more than 20 push-ups with no problem, completes medicine ball tosses using 20-pound weights, and leg presses 70 pounds.

7. You know someone is tough when they have beaten cancer, not just once but four different times. In January 2020, RBG announced she was cancer-free after she beat her fourth battle with cancer.

8. Four grandchildren are lucky enough to call Ginsburg *"Bubbie."* One of Ginsburg's grandchildren, Clara, followed in her footsteps; she recently graduated from Harvard Law School.

9. Ginsburg was the first Supreme Court Justice to preside over a same-sex wedding.

10. As accomplished and successful as she is, RBG is just not a morning person. She has stated that getting to work by 9:30 a.m. is difficult. It just goes to show you don't need to be a morning person to be an accomplished person.

CHAPTER 5:

HEDY LAMARR

Hedy Lamarr is best known for her pretty face, but she was so much more. It's rare to be gorgeous beyond belief and genius-level smart, and Hedy was both of those things. Not only was she so beautiful that she starred in Hollywood films with Clark Gable, but in her spare time, she invented communication technology, which led to today's Wi-Fi, GPS, and Bluetooth.

Hedy Lamarr was born Hedwig Eva Maria Kiesler on November 9, 1914, in Vienna, Austria. She was an only child, born into a wealthy Jewish family. She spent a great deal of time with her father, who encouraged her to look at the way the world worked from an early age. The two would take walks, and he would explain how things worked, from printing presses to streetcars. By age five, Hedy could already disassemble and reassemble her music box.

When she was young, Hedy attended private school in Vienna, where her favorite subject was chemistry. Her family was also particularly cultured and spent their free time taking Hedy to the opera and the theater. Later in life, she said how much she missed Austria and the culture she experienced there.

Even though she showed early signs of brilliance, Hedy's beauty is what people recognized. She eventually succumbed to this focus, and it led to her acting career. Her first small role was in a film called *Geld auf der Straße*, which translates to *"Money on the Street."* But it wasn't until two years later when she starred in the film, *Ecstasy*, that she became known across the world, not only for her beauty but for the controversial movie itself.

Hedy was only 18 when she starred in *Ecstasy*, in 1933. The film caused an uproar around the world because it had nude sex scenes and a female orgasm. Although sex scenes are typical today, this was the first non-pornographic film to have a naked sex scene. People were even more riled up because of how young Hedy was. *Ecstasy* caused such an enormous fuss that it was denounced by the Pope, forbidden by Hitler, and even banned in the United States.

It was through her acting career that Hedy met her first husband, Friedrich *"Fritz"* Mandl. He saw Hedy perform in a play called *Sissy* and adored her straight away. Fritz was a munitions tycoon from Austria, often described as the *"Henry Ford of Austria."* He was 14 years older than Hedy and was allied with the Nazis. The two married in 1933, but the marriage didn't last long.

Fritz was an extremely jealous person and always thought that Hedy was having an affair. He would even instruct their maids to listen in on her phone calls. Hedy was extremely unhappy in their marriage and claimed that he treated her like his pretty arm piece. She also couldn't stand the company she had to entertain, which frequently included members of the Nazi party.

In 1937, Hedy took extreme measures to escape Fritz. First, she took control of hiring the household's maids and hired a maid who resembled her. One night, during a dinner party, she put sleeping powder in a cup and switched it with the maid's cup. She loaded herself up with all her jewels, put on the maid's uniform, and took off on her bicycle.

She fled to London, where, after seeing an MGM movie, she set out to find an American film agent. Although Hedy couldn't even speak English at the time, she got an introduction to Louis B. Mayer, who was scouting for actresses to work for MGM Studios. Many young women were fleeing Europe at the time. Mayer offered Hedy $125.00/week to sign on with him. Although she had no other opportunities at the time, Hedy tried to bargain with him for more money. When he said no, she simply walked out.

One of the most badass facts about Hedy is that she rarely settled, and took her destiny into her hands, time after time. She wasn't about to give up after she met with Louise B. Mayer. She found out Mayer was heading back to America on the ship, the *Normandie*, so she booked her passage on the same boat.

One night, she dressed up in a gorgeous, couture gown and strode into the ballroom. All eyes were on her, including Louise B. Mayer's. He made her another offer of $500.00/week, and she gladly accepted. The only stone left unturned was the issue of her name, as it did not sound very fashionable to Americans. Mayer's wife came up with *"Lamarr."* When she stepped off the *Normandie* in America to the flashing of cameras, Hedwig Eva Kiesler had become Hedy Lamarr.

Despite her beauty, Lamarr didn't become a star instantly. Her initial time in Hollywood left her feeling insecure because she wasn't getting any suitable roles. That all changed when she went to a party with a famous actor, Charles Boyer, and ended up starring in *Algiers* with him. *Algiers* became an instant hit, and Lamarr's beauty was its main drawcard. It was so successful that it even inspired the classic film, *Casablanca*. That movie's starring role was written for Lamarr.

After starring in *Algiers*, Hedy Lamarr was an *"It Girl"* in Hollywood. She was on the cover of every popular magazine and began to meet all the *"greats,"* from John F. Kennedy to

Picasso. Lamarr had the opportunity to meet many influential people, one of whom became a significant influence in her life.

Howard Hughes, the famous pilot, was the first person in a long time to recognize Lamarr's intellectual brilliance and encouraged her to innovate. He even gave her a chemistry set she could use in her trailer on her Hollywood sets.

It is surprising that Lamarr even had the time to invent, considering the success of her acting career. Hollywood was a grueling industry at the time, particularly for female actresses. Many of them had contracts binding them to their studio's *"shortlist"* for seven years. They worked six days a week, often long into the night. Many of the actresses were given pills to stay awake—most often speed—and then sleeping pills to go to bed. Even though Lamarr spent a great deal of her time on set in Hollywood, she couldn't stop the inventive gears from turning in her brain.

Howard Hughes took Lamarr to the factories he owned so that she could see how his planes were constructed. Hughes told her of his plans to make his planes faster so they could be of use to the military, and Lamarr was inspired to look into it further. She found her inspiration in birds and fish, attempting to understand the fastest of both species. She cleverly used this information to sketch new designs for plane wings. It was after this that Hughes fully recognized her true genius. Once Lamarr got started inventing, she didn't stop. She created an improved stoplight and a tablet that could be dissolved in water to make a soda that tasted like Coca-Cola.

During World War II, Lamarr spent her time thinking about a

way to turn the tide in Britain's favor. The German U-boats seemed unsinkable and were inflicting significant damage to the Allies and innocent civilians trying to cross the seas. Lamarr wanted to use her inventive mind to think of something to make a difference. She didn't want to just sit on the sidelines; she even contemplated quitting her acting career numerous times to pursue science instead.

It was around this time, in 1940, that Lamarr met George Antheil at a dinner party. The two clicked right away. Lamarr and Antheil both felt misunderstood in life and wanted to do something more. They spent a lot of time talking about the war. Both predicted that America would be joining the war effort very soon. Lamarr was a patriotic American and she wanted Hitler dead. She also had a vast knowledge of weapons and war that she gained while married to the munitions dealer back in Austria. Antheil's motivations came from his brother, who was killed at the start of World War II. He wanted revenge for his brother's death.

Lamarr and Antheil worked together on three inventions aimed at helping the Allies beat the Germans. One ended up being one of the most important inventions of the century. Lamarr had been thinking about designing something that could secretly guide torpedoes to their targets. She had the idea of creating a frequency-hopping system so that the signal couldn't be tracked or jammed. Like Lamarr, Antheil didn't have engineering training, but he did have a solid understanding of synchronizing pianos. So, he worked on synchronizing a player-piano with radio signals.

This pair of untrained scientists eventually completed groundbreaking work in frequency-hopping that formed the basis for the wireless communications that followed including Bluetooth, Wi-Fi, and GPS. Once they had enough information to show their invention to others, Lamarr and Antheil presented it to the National Inventors Council, who linked them up with a physicist. Shortly after, they patented their design and gave it to the United States Navy so they could use it to help them win the war against the Axis powers. Despite its brilliance, the navy turned down the system. To add insult to injury, the navy told Lamarr she should utilize her fame and beauty to raise money for the war efforts instead of inventing. She wanted to continue developing the invention, but Antheil disagreed. Although Lamarr felt rejected, she still wanted to do good for her adopted country and decided to help by selling war bonds.

Lamarr went on tour to convince people to buy more bonds. At every stop, she picked a sailor from the crowd and told everyone that she'd kiss the sailor if everyone attending the show bought a war bond. The *"random"* sailor was, in fact, a man called Eddie Rhodes who was part of her routine. Together, they raised what would be $340 million today.

Lamarr she decided she wanted to start producing her own movies and—despite discouragement from others—that's exactly what she did. This was unheard of at the time. Lamarr didn't call herself a feminist, but that's precisely what she was. She started her production studio in 1946, the only woman to do so besides Bette Davis. Lamarr produced and starred in two noir films, *The Strange Woman* and *Dishonored Lady*.

After World War II, Lamarr got married for the third time. She wanted a family and a home, and she married actor John Loder, and they had two children together. Ultimately, he was too dull for her, and she ended up living as a single mother in her 40s. Her children remember her as a warm and loving mother during this time. She taught them how to swim and worked as hard as she could to support them all. Despite her poor financial situation, Lamarr also paid for her mother to move to California at this time.

In 1949, she had a stroke of good luck, starring in the Paramount Pictures hit, *Samson and Delilah*, which was the second highest-grossing film of the entire decade. Many say this film was Lamarr's greatest success in the film industry. In 1954, she produced a film in a similar style, *Loves of Three Queens*. Lamarr poured millions into the project and lost all her money.

In 1953, Lamarr married her fifth husband, Howard Lee, who was an oilman from Texas. She and her children moved to Texas, where she found herself a trophy wife again. The two started going on ski trips, and Lamarr fell in love with Colorado. She poured her efforts into building an Austrian style ski resort in Aspen, Colorado, and named it *"Villa LaMarr."*

Howard Lee was an alcoholic, and the relationship fell apart. Lamarr went through one of the darkest times of her life when her son was almost killed in a car accident. She was such a wreck that she sent her Hollywood body double to testify for her in divorce court. The judge was furious, and Lamarr got nothing in the divorce settlement. She lost the only thing she had wanted: her beloved Villa LaMarr.

Hedy's children remember her starting to act erratically and being extremely unstable around this time. Her status as a patient of the famous Dr. Feelgood could explain her behavior. A lot of stars, and the rich and famous—including John F. Kennedy and Jackie Kennedy—were patients of Dr. Feelgood. Lamarr became his patient sometime in the 1950s and continued seeing him until the 1970s when he lost his license. She became hooked on Dr. Feelgood's *"vitamins."* His special vitamin elixirs contained roughly 40 milligrams of methamphetamines; they were extremely addictive.

Lamarr's children claimed that these *"vitamins"* turned her into an absolute monster. While she was suffering from her addiction, Lamarr started shoplifting and was arrested twice, though she was never convicted for the crimes. She had won a role in a new movie but lost it because of the petty crimes.

In 1969, Lamarr wrote to a friend in the navy asking what had happened to her invention, but it was too late. There is evidence suggesting the navy did use her invention, but sadly, Lamarr's patent had expired. She never earned a dime for her creation, even though the navy likely used it when the patent was still active. Lamarr's invention became the basis for Bluetooth, Wi-Fi, GPS, and other wireless communications upon which our modern world depends today. She continued to make money as an actress, but she wasn't recognized in any way for her incredible contributions to science.

As Lamarr aged, she became more and more self-conscious. She began getting plastic surgery at age 40 and never stopped. In the 1970s, she started receding from public life. Lamarr was offered some TV commercials and scripts but didn't want to do any of them. In 1981, once her eyesight started failing, she moved to Miami, Florida.

The public was never aware that Lamarr was more than a movie star until a journalist, Fleming Meeks, released an article about her in *Forbes* in 1990. Throughout the 1990s, Lamarr finally began to be recognized for her scientific work.

In 1997, the Electronic Frontier Foundation awarded Lamarr and Antheil with their Pioneer Award. Lamarr's son accepted her award on her behalf. She also went on to become the first woman to ever receive the BULBIE Gnass Spirit of Achievement Award from the Inventor's Convention, considered the Oscars of inventing.

Sadly, by the time Lamarr finally began to be acknowledged for her brilliant mind—which she had wanted all of her life—she was living as a recluse in Florida. She didn't attend any of her award ceremonies. She only communicated over the phone, and never visited with people in person, including her children and her closest friends.

Lamarr died from heart disease on January 19, 2000, at the age of 85. At her request, her son, Anthony Loder, spread her ashes in the Vienna Woods. Her homeland remained dear to her until the end of her days.

It wasn't until 14 years after her death that Hedy Lamarr was finally inducted into the National Inventors Hall of Fame. Lamarr is now known as *"the mother of Wi-Fi."*

HEDY LAMARR: DID YOU KNOW?

1. Hedy Lamarr was the model for the animated Disney movie, *Snow White*, and the inspiration behind DC Comics' Catwoman.

2. In 1966, Lamarr published a best-selling autobiography entitled *Ecstasy and Me*. However, she ended up suing her publisher because there were numerous misrepresentations in the book, which was written by a ghostwriter.

3. Lamarr was the first person to act out an on-screen orgasm in a regular non-pornographic film.

4. In 2004, a documentary, *Calling Hedy Lamarr*, was released. It featured her children, Denise Loder-DeLuca and Anthony Loder.

5. Lamarr was never impressed with her beauty. She was quoted numerous times stating, *"Any girl can be glamorous; all you have to do is stand still and look stupid."*

6. In 1960, Lamarr was awarded a star on the Hollywood Walk of Fame for her many contributions to the film industry.

7. Lamarr dated many famous men, including John F. Kennedy, before he became the President of the United States. John F. Kennedy asked her out on a date, and when he asked what he could bring her, she said she wanted oranges because she needed Vitamin C.

8. Lamarr's first husband, Friedrich *"Fritz"* Mandl, was an insanely jealous person. After he married Lamarr, he went on a hunt to destroy every single copy of *Ecstasy* that existed. Fritz spent what would be millions today buying copies of the film to destroy it; he never succeeded.

9. Lamarr was meant to star as Ilsa in the classic movie, *Casablanca*, but she couldn't get permission from MGM to star in a Warner Brothers film. The role went to Ingrid Bergman instead.

10. In 2017, a documentary was made about Lamarr's life beyond her time as an actress. The film is called *Bombshell: The Hedy Lamarr Story*.

CHAPTER 6:

FRIDA KAHLO

What do badass women do when they face adversity? They not only survive, they also thrive. To say that Frida Kahlo faced adversity in her life is an understatement, yet still, she became one of the greatest Mexican artists of all time.

Frida Kahlo was born in Coyoacán, Mexico, on July 6, 1907, to a German father and an Amerindian and Spanish mother. Her father was also an artist—a photographer—and Frida was always close to him.

When Frida was just six years old, she contracted polio and was bedridden for nine months. She recovered but always had a limp and wore long skirts to hide it for the rest of her life. Frida always marched to the beat of a different drum and was true to herself. Politics became an essential part of Frida's life, and later, her art. She joined the Communist Party in the 1920s and remained active in politics for the remainder of her years.

While attending the National Preparatory School in Mexico City, she became known for being daring and outspoken. She embraced a group of fellow students who called themselves the *"Cachuchas."* They had similar left-leaning political and intellectual ideas. One of the group's members, Alejandro Gómez Arias, became Frida's first serious relationship and he was with her on one of the most tragic days of her short life.

One day when they were still students, Frida and Alejandro were on a bus when it collided with an oncoming electric streetcar. A steel handrail impaled Frida's hip. She fractured her spine and pelvis, dislocated her shoulder, and broke her collarbone. Additionally, her right leg was broken in 11 different places. Frida spent about a month in the Red Cross Hospital in Mexico City, undergoing numerous surgeries. When she was released from hospital, Frida returned home for what turned out to be a long recovery.

Put in a full body cast for three months, plagued with insufferable pain, Frida Kahlo started working on her art in bed, primarily on her cast. Her parents got her an easel so she could continue to paint in bed more comfortably. It was during this time that Kahlo began what became a series of self-portraits. She did these by hanging a mirror on the canopy of her bed. Kahlo remained her own muse for her art, stating, *"I am my own muse. I am the subject I know best. The subject I want to better."*

Kahlo endured more than 30 surgeries after her injury. Despite slim odds, she did walk again. She felt obligated to support her parents; she thought that her injury had been a burden to them. She wanted a realistic and professional opinion of her art to see if she could make a living as an artist. Kahlo decided to seek out the opinion of the famous Mexican artist and muralist, Diego Rivera, who she had a brief encounter with during her time as a student.

Diego admired Kahlo's painting and encouraged her to continue. Shortly after meeting, the two began a relationship, which would last for the rest of Kahlo's life. The two had a 20-year age difference, but that didn't bother them. Not only did they share a common interest in art, they both shared the same political views: they were comrades for life. Despite Kahlo's mother's disapproval, they got married in August of 1929.

Kahlo and Rivera's marriage was not a typical one. Rivera was a well-known womanizer and frequently had affairs with other women. Kahlo was aware of this going into their union and had some affairs of her own. The couple also kept separate homes and studios for most of their marriage. Despite all this, their deep love for each other was undeniable.

Early on in their marriage, the couple moved around a lot for Rivera's work: San Francisco in 1930, New York for Rivera's Museum of Modern Art show in 1931, and then Detroit for Rivera's work with the Detroit Institute of Arts in 1932.

While in Detroit, on July 4, 1932, Frida suffered a miscarriage, a scene she depicted in her famous painting, *"Henry Ford Hospital."* Kahlo had several miscarriages due to the injuries she sustained in the bus accident. She eventually had to grapple with the fact that she would be unable to have children. Later scientific research has found that Kahlo suffered from Asherman's syndrome—intrauterine scarring— due to the bus accident.

By 1933, the couple was back in New York City. Rivera had been commissioned by the rich and famous family, the Rockefellers, to paint a mural at the Rockefeller Center. Titled *"Man at the Crossroads,"* the painting sparked controversy because it depicted communist leader Vladimir Lenin. Rockefeller halted Rivera's work, and this ended the couple's time in the United States. They returned to Mexico, which Kahlo was happy about because she never liked the U.S.

After Kahlo and Rivera returned to Mexico, the couple still resided in separate residences. Rivera continued to have affairs, but the one that caused Kahlo real anguish was his affair with Kahlo's sister, Cristina. In response, Kahlo chopped off all her hair and experienced a period of depression.

In the late 1930s, Kahlo befriended André Breton, a significant figure in the Surrealist movement. Frida's career started to take off around the same year that she met Breton. In 1938, she had an exhibition in New York City where she commissioned two paintings.

In 1939, Kahlo took an opportunity to move to Paris to pursue her art. Paris, during this time, was full of great artists, and she became friends with Pablo Picasso, Marc Chagall, and Piet Mondrian.

Another significant life event occurred during Kahlo's stay in Paris: her divorce from Rivera. To represent the divorce, she painted one of her most famous paintings, *"The Two Fridas,"* while still living in Paris. When Frida returned to Mexico in 1940, she remarried Rivera. They still lived separate lives and continued to have affairs with other people.

In 1941, Kahlo was commissioned by the Mexican government to paint five portraits of important Mexican women. Unfortunately, faced with numerous personal issues, she was never able to finish. Kahlo's father, to whom she had remained close, passed away. Her health also continued to deteriorate. In 1944, she depicted her constant pain and the physical challenges she was facing in one of her most famous portraits, *"The Broken Column."* In the painting, her spine is shattered, and she's split down the middle, wearing a brace, with nails throughout her body. During this time of excruciating pain, Kahlo sought numerous treatments, but nothing helped to ease her chronic pain.

Despite everything, Kahlo carried on with her life and continued to paint. In 1950, her health took an extreme turn for the worst, and she was diagnosed with gangrene in her right foot. She underwent several surgeries and was bedridden for nine months. Still, she persisted and continued to paint, even though she was confined to a wheelchair.

In 1953, Kahlo finally had a solo exhibition in her home country of Mexico. Shortly after the show, she had to undergo another surgery—this time to have her right leg amputated below the knee, to stop the gangrene. She was in constant pain and suffered bouts of depression during this difficult time.

Kahlo could have given up, and most people would have. But despite her severe health condition, she continued to paint. She even remained active in the political movement, attending a protest against the United States backing of the overthrow of President Jacobo Árbenz of Guatemala. This protest was Kahlo's final public appearance before her death. She died due to a pulmonary embolism on July 13, 1954, at the young age of 47.

Frida Kahlo's work didn't reach the height of its fame until two decades after her death. She became an icon of the feminist movement in the 1970s. While she was alive, Frida Kahlo was often only known as *"Diego Rivera's wife."* Now, the tide has changed, and Diego Rivera is known as *"Frida Kahlo's husband."*

FRIDA KAHLO: DID YOU KNOW?

1. After she recovered from polio as a child, Kahlo's father convinced her to participate in lots of sports, including wrestling, swimming, and soccer; not at all typical of a girl in the early 20th century!

2. A movie was made about Kahlo's life in 2002, starring Salma Hayek. The film, titled *Frida*, was nominated for six Academy Awards and won two, for Best Makeup and Best Original Score.

3. Kahlo was not only bisexual, she was open about it, which was way ahead of her time. During her turbulent marriage, in which Rivera had numerous affairs, Kahlo had relations with both men and women. Kahlo is rumored to have had affairs with multiple women, including artists Georgia O'Keefe and Josephine Baker.

4. Kahlo's actual birthday was July 6, 1907, but when asked, she would often tell people that her birth date was July 7, 1910. She wanted her birthday to be associated with the Mexican Revolution.

5. Kahlo's face is on one side of the Mexican 500 peso note. On the other side of the bill? Diego Rivera!

6. The Louvre in Paris bought Kahlo's painting, *"The Frame,"* in 1939, making Frida the first 20th-century Mexican artist to have a painting purchased by an internationally renowned museum.

7. When Leon Trotsky, the Leader of the Red Army, moved to Mexico after getting political asylum from the Soviet Union, he stayed at the *"Blue House"* with Kahlo and Rivera. Allegedly, Kahlo and Trotsky had an affair during that time.

8. Kahlo's house, Casa Azul, where she was born and died, is now a museum and major tourist attraction, containing numerous works by Kahlo and Rivera.

9. Kahlo waited her whole life to have a solo exhibition in her home country of Mexico. When the day finally came, in 1953, her health was so poor that doctors advised her to stay home. Kahlo decided she couldn't miss the exhibition. She arrived by ambulance and had her bed towed on a truck, so she could be placed on her bed and carried into the show by four men.

10. Throughout her life, Kahlo defied stereotypes and was true to herself. She is known for rocking a unibrow and a mustache for her entire life. Her sometimes androgynous style—including wearing men's suits—also challenged the norms of the times.

CHAPTER 7:

HUDA SHA'ARAWI

Huda Sha'arawi was the first woman to publicly defy Egypt's order that women must wear a veil in public, an act that took more bravery than many people possess. Egypt's first feminist, Sha'arawi is most known for this unveiling; however, she accomplished so much more than that for the women of the Middle East.

Born in Cairo, Egypt, in 1879, Huda Sha'arawi had a wealthy family and a relatively happy childhood. Muhammad Sultan

Pasha, Huda's father, was the first president of the Egyptian Representative Council, and her mother, Iqbal, was a Circassian refugee who was brought over to Egypt when she was a young girl.

During her early childhood, Huda had the freedom to play and explore in the open air, defying the restrictions often placed on young girls. She spent a great deal of time playing with her brother, Umar Sultan. Her father made plenty of time to play with his children, and she recalls him bringing them home chocolates.

Sadly, when Huda was five, her father passed away, and she mourned his death deeply. As her childhood resumed, though, she still enjoyed a certain degree of freedom. She learned to play the piano, read books in her father's library, and dedicated time to learning languages, becoming fluent in Arabic, Turkish, and French. Huda enjoyed spending time in the garden learning about horticulture from the family's gardener, Matta, and a slave called Anbar. She also learned calligraphy, painting, music, and poetry.

However, at nine years old, Huda began to lose the freedoms that she had always enjoyed. Huda was raised in the harem system, which kept women entirely separate from men. Wealthy families had separate buildings or apartments where all the women of the household were isolated. The women's housing was often guarded by eunuchs—castrated males—who would take messages out for the women; that was how rarely they went into public. When they did, they were always veiled. Huda started having to spend more and more time in the harem.

Born into a society where women had little to no control over whom they married and when, Huda was just 13 years old when her parents arranged a marriage to her older cousin, Ali Sha'arawi. He was 26 years Huda's senior and was appointed as her legal guardian if her father died. She didn't want to marry and tried to refuse her parents but was unsuccessful.

Huda's marriage contract stated that her husband had to leave his slave-concubine, but shortly after they were married, the slave-concubine had his child. As a result, Huda was able to leave him for seven years. Because her father was also dead, Huda had a rare degree of freedom after she left her husband. She was able to further her education and became an activist during this time.

Huda also had the opportunity to travel and observe the freedom and independence exercised by European women. She took vacations to the Mediterranean and interacted with numerous well-educated women, whose freedoms made her discontent about her situation even stronger.

During her time of freedom, Huda also met one of her most significant life influences, Eugénie Le Brun, a French woman who had married an Egyptian man. Eugénie hosted weekly gatherings, which Huda attended, and the women would often talk about social practices and customs. Eugénie is the one who initially brought up the subject of the veil, which she saw as hindering the advancement of Egyptian women. This would play a large part in Huda's motives later on in her life.

When she was 21 years old, Huda Sha'arawi reunited with her husband, Ali Sha'arawi, and had two children, Bathna and Muhammad. Ali was a political activist as well, and many observed that, when the couple got back together, they appeared to have a marriage based on equality. He frequently sought her advice and invited her to high-level political meetings.

In 1908, Sha'arawi started the first charity organization run by women in Egypt. It focused on assisting poor Egyptian women and children. The organization even offered classes in infant care, family hygiene, and household management.

Sha'arawi believed strongly in the importance of women-run social service agencies for several reasons. She recognized the importance of women gaining practical knowledge and focusing on projects outside of the home or the harem. Sha'arawi thought it sent an important message that women do not need protection and that they are not merely *"creatures of pleasure."*

In 1910, Sha'arawi opened a school for girls that focused on academics. Previously, schools for girls in Egypt focused on practical skills such as midwifery. She started organizing and getting women in Egypt into the public sphere. She began by presenting lectures, first by visiting women, and eventually, by Egyptian women. In 1914, Marguerite Clement agreed to do a lecture when she was visiting Egypt. The lectures evolved into the founding of the Intellectual Association of Egyptian Women in 1914.

Like all people, even heroes, Sha'arawi struggled with her own battles, primarily with her mental health. She suffered from numerous bouts of depression, or *"melancholy,"* as it was called at the time. Her first severe depression came after the loss of her mother and then her brother, Umar, a few years later. She left her home in Cairo and recovered in Minya, her second home built for her by her husband. Sha'arawi suffered depressive episodes at various times throughout her life, including after the loss of her close friend Eugénie. During such times, she was unable to eat, smoked obsessively, and became paranoid about the health of her children.

Following World War I, more and more Egyptian women started leaving the harem to participate in organized political protests against the British for Egyptian independence. A known nationalist, Sha'arawi was responsible for organizing the largest women's anti-British political demonstration in Egypt at the time. In 1919, the women stood in protest in the heat of the sun for hours, despite the British orders to disband. In 1920, Sha'arawi was appointed the president of the Wafidist Women's Central Committee, a committee organized to coordinate women's political activities in Egypt's independence movement, a position she held until 1924.

Egypt gained its independence from Great Britain in 1922. The newly independent government wanted women to return to the harem system; yes, even after they had worked so hard to liberate their country! Women in Egypt were further outraged when the government also denied women's suffrage. The government then proceeded to ban women from the opening of the new Egyptian Parliament. In response, Sha'arawi led a group of women to picket the event. The women protesters issued a list of 32 demands.

Sha'arawi didn't just protest the new government's treatment of women; she started taking drastic measures to take control over her own life and make a statement for what she believed was right. In 1923, Sha'arawi did something that had never been done before.

Sha'arawi had attended an international conference on woman suffrage, and after disembarking from her train in Cairo on her way home, she made the bold decision to remove her veil. People were shocked and then started applauding her; some even removed their veils as well.

This was the first time that someone had publicly removed their veil. By challenging this restrictive tradition, Sha'arawi inspired other women to refuse to wear their veils as well. Within a few decades, few women in Egypt were wearing the veil.

Sha'arawi also helped found the Egyptian Feminist Union (EFU) and was the president of the organization for 24 years until her death. The EFU campaigned to raise the minimum legal age for women to marry to 16, fought for girls' right to education, and advocated for women's suffrage.

Two of the organization's biggest wins occurred in 1927 and 1933. In 1927, the first secondary school for Egyptian girls was founded following pressure from the EFU. Additionally, in 1933, parliament established new work laws for women, requiring employers to adhere to a maximum nine-hour workday, one month of maternity leave, and 15 days of leave at 50% of their salary after having a child.

Not only did Sha'arawi fight for women's equality in Egypt, she also attended international conferences and spoke up for peace and equality for women everywhere. One of Sha'arawi's goals in founding the EFU was to send a delegation of women from Egypt to represent their country at the 9th Congress of the International Women's Suffrage Alliance in Rome, in 1923.

Sha'arawi and her delegation were able to attend, and she gave a riveting feminist speech about women in Egypt. Her argument on behalf of the rights of Egyptian women was founded on the fact that in ancient Egypt women were equal to men, one of the earliest civilizations to have that status. It was only when foreign powers dominated the country that women lost their rights. Sha'arawi also argued that, in Islam, women and men are granted equal rights; to her, the issue wasn't Islam but the misinterpretation of the Koran.

Later in life, Sha'arawi was faced with significant health problems, primarily with her heart. However, she didn't let this stop her from continuing her life as an activist and a feminist. She didn't slow down as she aged. She became a member of the International Alliance of Women for Suffrage and Equal Citizenship, serving as its vice-president in 1935. In 1938, Sha'arawi worked with the EFU to sponsor the Eastern Women's Conference for the Defense of Palestine in Cairo, signaling her prioritization of nationalist concerns. She also founded the Arab Feminist Union in 1945.

Throughout her life, Sha'arawi continued to travel and represent Egyptian women at congresses and conferences around the world, in Paris, Amsterdam, Berlin, Marseilles, Istanbul, Brussels, Budapest, Copenhagen, Graz, and Geneva. Sha'arawi worked for peace and equality until she died of a heart attack in 1947. Even on her deathbed, she was in the process of writing to the governments of the Arab world, asking them to stand against the UN decision to divide Palestine.

Most prominent in Huda Sha'arawi's vast legacy is the groundwork she laid for the Egyptian women's liberation movement, a struggle that continues today.

HUDA SHA'ARAWI: DID YOU KNOW?

1. Sha'arawi was not only an activist, she was also an author. Her book, *Harem Years: The Memoirs of an Egyptian Feminist*, published in 1987, gave outsiders a real account of what it was like to live in the private world of a harem in Cairo. It was told from her perspective as a member of one of the last generations to live in a harem in Egypt.

2. Sha'arawi led the first women's street demonstration ever held in Egypt, during the Egyptian Revolution of 1919.

3. Iqbal Hanim, Sha'arawi's mother, was not the legitimate wife of Sha'arawi's father. It was common during the harem years for upper-class Egyptian men to have not just a wife, but concubines, who were also known as *"second wives."* Her mother was her father's concubine, and they lived together in the harem with her father's wife, Hasiba, and his other children. Sha'arawi often confided in Hasiba, who she called, *"Umm Kariba,"* meaning *"Big Mother."*

4. The Egyptian Feminist Union published Egypt's first feminist magazine, *l'Egyptienne* (later known as *el-Masreyya*), under Sha'arawi's leadership.

5. In 1914, Sha'arawi founded the Intellectual Association of Egyptian Women.

6. Sha'arawi directed a play, *Lutfia al-Nadi*, based on the first

Egyptian—as well as Arab—woman to earn her pilot's license.

7. When she was just a young girl, Sha'arawi memorized parts of the Koran, which was unusual for girls. She felt frustrated because no one had ever formally taught her Arabic, so she couldn't understand what she memorized. She asked for Arabic grammar lessons so she could understand the meaning of the Koran and was denied. She was told girls didn't need to know those things. She later learned with the help of female tutors in Cairo.

8. Sha'arawi claims in her memoirs that a huge source of her inspiration in life came from a female poet, Sayyida Khadija al-Maghribiyya, who used to come to her family home. She watched the poet being able to freely communicate with the men in her household and realized that educated women could be seen as equal to men.

9. The Egyptian President, Gamal Abdel Nasser, was so threatened by Sha'arawi's ideas that, following her death, he banned the women's movement that she had started. Nasser co-opted Sha'arawi's legacy to promote a state-approved brand of feminism that, in reality, gave Egyptian women few rights. Unfortunately, autocratic rule in Egypt over many decades has eroded many of Sha'arawi's hard-won gains, but the fight continues.

10. In 1945, Sha'arawi was awarded Egypt's highest honor that a woman can receive, Nishan al-Kamal, which means *"Order of the Virtues."*

CHAPTER 8:

NANCY WAKE

Nancy Wake was a fearless fighter and one of the greatest war heroines of all time. Not many women in the 1940s spent their time killing members of the Gestapo with their bare hands or marching 7,000 male resistance fighters through the woods to liberate France. Nancy Wake lived her life as a badass until the end of her days.

Nancy Wake was born in Wellington, New Zealand on August 30, 1912. She was the youngest of six siblings and was born into an impoverished family. When she was a baby, her family relocated to Sydney, Australia, where she lived until she was 16 years old.

As a teenager, Nancy attended the North Sydney Household Arts School, and at the young age of 16, she decided to run away from home to become a nurse. After nursing for a few years, she then worked for a shipping company, all the while dreaming of adventure.

In 1932, Wake inherited a small amount of money from an aunt and was finally able to travel to Europe to start a new life. First, she resided in London, where she studied journalism. She then settled in Paris and started working as a journalist.

In her work as a reporter, Wake traveled to Vienna and Berlin. Fascism was on the rise and, in the beautiful city of Vienna, Wake witnessed the brutal treatment of the Jewish people by German soldiers. She was appalled. What she saw immediately turned her into a staunch opponent of the Nazis. She decided then: if she ever had the opportunity to fight against them, she was going to take it.

Shortly before Germany invaded France, Wake married Henri Fiocca, a wealthy French businessman, in Marseilles. Six months later, Germany invaded France, and Wake got her opportunity to get involved. She started by driving an ambulance. Soon, Wake and her husband joined the French Resistance, helping Jewish refugees and Allied servicemen—such as pilots who were downed—get from safe house to safe house across France. They would smuggle refugees across the state until they reached the Pyrenees mountains, where the desperate people could be smuggled into Spain.

Nancy Wake infamously became known by the Gestapo as the *"White Mouse"* because she always managed to evade their clutches. At one point, the Gestapo had Wake on their most-wanted list and a bounty of five million francs for her capture. They became so dedicated to finding her that they even started searching her mail and staking out her home; still, they failed again and again.

In 1943, Wake was finally captured and interrogated by the Germans for four days. She successfully escaped from their grasp one last time, via the same route through which she had led the refugees, through the Pyrenees Mountains. She traveled through Spain alone and ended up in England. She had to leave her husband behind in France.

Wake's courage and intelligence regarding the enemy in France were seen to be of great value to England, so they recruited her to join the French Section of the Special Operations Executive (SOE) in 1943. She underwent training and learned how to break codes, blow up bridges, and kill people with her bare hands, a skill she needed later in her life on the front.

After her training, Wake bravely parachuted into France, where Captain Henri Tardivat, of the French Resistance, happened to discover her. She had become tangled in a tree after parachuting from the sky out of a B-24 bomber. Wake was in a rush and was carrying critical classified documents. The captain, under the impression that she was a beautiful damsel in distress, remarked, *"I hope that all the trees in France bear such beautiful fruit this year."* Wake responded, *"Don't give me that French shit."* She didn't need saving; she promptly untangled herself out of the tree and carried on with her duties.

While working for the SOE in France, Wake was responsible for organizing and leading over 7,000 male resistance fighters for D-Day assaults. Many may wonder how a beautiful woman gained the respect of thousands of men in war, and if they bothered to follow her orders. Her method, though perhaps unorthodox, was highly effective—she used whiskey. She would bring out a bottle of whiskey and drink the men under the table until dawn. When the night was over, they were ready to follow her orders.

Wake wasn't just a drinker either; she was a fearless force to be reckoned with in hand-to-hand combat. She is known for numerous courageous acts during the war. One of the most infamous occurred when the SOE was breaking into a gun factory. An SS soldier caught them and was about to give them away when Wake killed the German guard with a swift karate chop to the neck. She also ordered the execution of a female French spy, whom men in the French Resistance were too hesitant to execute. Wake saw espionage as an act of war, and she was willing to do what was needed regardless of gender, with the rationale that the enemy would do the same to her.

Although these are impressive feats, Nancy didn't see it that way. She was most proud of biking for 310 miles, through roadblocks and Nazi checkpoints, to deliver radio codes to the Allies. The journey took her about 72 hours, and she was able to restore communications for the Resistance after her journey.

Toward the end of the war, Wake discovered that her husband had been killed by the Gestapo. He had been tortured because he refused to disclose her location. Henri had been the great love of her life, and she mourned deeply, feeling responsible for his death.

After the war, Wake was recognized for her courage and her service to the allies. She was one of the most decorated women of World War II, receiving the George Medal from Britain, the Medal of Freedom from the United States, and the Croix de Guerre and Resistance Medal from France. At 92 years old, she was finally decorated by her own country, Australia, when she was named a member of the Order of Australia.

When the war was over, Wake didn't just sit back; she decided she wanted to pursue a new venture and run for Parliament in Australia. She was unsuccessful in her 1949 run for Parliament, but she didn't let that stop her from trying again. She ran again in 1951 and still didn't win.

Wake decided to return to England in the 1950s and resume work with British Intelligence. It was back in England where she met her second husband, John Melvin Forward, who had been an English fighter pilot.

In 1985, Wake became an author and published an autobiography, *The White Mouse,* which became a bestseller. Shortly after the publication of her book, Wake and her husband moved back to Australia.

After 40 long years of marriage, her husband passed away on August 19, 1997, and Wake decided she wanted to live out the remainder of her days back in Europe. To fund her new life, she decided to sell her war medals, stating, *"I'll probably go to hell, and they'd melt anyway."*

At the age of 88, she packed up and moved into the Stafford Hotel in London, where she became a staple of the establishment. People would find her having a couple of drinks at the hotel bar. She became such a beloved regular that the bar set aside a special chair for her in the corner. If someone dared to sit in her special seat, she would ask them to move.

When Wake was no longer able to pay her hotel bill at the Stafford, Britain's royal family stepped in to help her. The Prince of Wales donated money from his trust to pay the bill for her hotel stay. Nancy lived most of the remainder of her days at the Stafford. In fact, her dying wish was to die there, but she died in a London hospital on August 7, 2011, at the age of 98.

Nancy is remembered today as one of the greatest war heroines of all time and the honorary resident badass of the Stafford Hotel in London.

NANCY WAKE: DID YOU KNOW?

1. At the beginning of her career, while Nancy Wake was freelancing for newspapers in Paris, she was sent on an assignment to interview someone in Vienna. That someone happened to be the new German Chancellor, Adolf Hitler.

2. Wake was invited to afternoon tea at Buckingham Palace with the Prince of Wales, where she gave him an autographed copy of her autobiography, *The White Mouse*.

3. A mini-series was released in 1987 based on the exploits of Nancy Wake. Filmed in Australia, it was called *Nancy Wake* and was based on the book by Russell Braddon, *Nancy Wake: The Story of a Very Brave Woman*.

4. Wake called herself a *"flirtatious little bastard,"* referring to her behavior when passing by German checkpoints. She would wink at the soldiers on duty and ask them if they wanted to search her. Naturally, they rarely did.

5. In 2002, artist Melissa Beowulf completed a portrait of Wake that was a finalist in the Doug Moran National Portrait Prize. The portrait has now been acquired by Australia's National Portrait Gallery.

6. Wake's obituary inspired many who hadn't heard her story before. It was included in—and formed the basis of the title of—a book of infamous *New York Times* obituaries

published in 2012, *The Socialite Who Killed a Nazi With Her Bare Hands: And 144 Other Fascinating People Who Died This Year.*

7. Wake's medals can now be found on display in the Second World War gallery at the Australian War Memorial Museum located in Canberra, Australia.

8. Wake participated in a badass raid that destroyed the headquarters of the SS in Montlucon and resulted in the death of 38 Germans.

9. In 2001, a bestselling biography of Nancy Wake, *A Biography of Our Greatest War Heroine,* was written and published by Australian author Peter FitzSimons.

10. One of Wake's fellow soldiers once described her as *"the most feminine woman I know until the fighting starts—then she is like five men."*

CHAPTER 9:

GERTRUDE BELL

Gertrude Bell's life story is so fascinating, it makes one wonder how someone could achieve and experience so much in just one lifetime. From scaling the Alps, learning seven languages, and helping establish what is modern-day Iraq, there is not much that Gertrude Bell didn't do in the inspiring life she led.

Born on July 14, 1868, into a wealthy family in England, Gertrude had the opportunity to receive an excellent education. It also opened her up to experiences and travels that many people couldn't have even dreamed of at that time. Early on in life, she was characterized as someone who sought out adventure, was fiercely independent, and had extremely high intellectual abilities.

Sadly, in 1871, when Gertrude was only three years old, her mother died while giving birth to her brother. As a result, Gertrude became extremely close to her father, Sir Hugh Bell, a progressive mill owner who believed in the fair treatment of his workers and held numerous government positions throughout his life. Without a doubt, Gertrude learned a great deal about politics from her father.

In her youth, Gertrude attended a prestigious girl's school, Queen's College, in London. At the young age of 17, she went on to study at Oxford. While at Oxford, she studied history at Lady Margaret Hall, which was one of the few colleges at Oxford that accepted women at the time. She became the first woman in Oxford's history to earn first-degree honors in her subject. Not only did Bell graduate with honors, she completed her college education in just two short years.

After graduating from Oxford, Bell spent her time pursuing her other passions such as travel, learning new languages, mountaineering, writing books, and conducting archaeological work. There seemed to be nothing she couldn't do.

Bell first fell in love with the Middle East in 1892, while visiting her uncle, Sir Frank Lascelles, in Iran (known then as Persia). He was the British ambassador to the region at the time, and Bell took her visit seriously. She didn't just go on a vacation; she voraciously studied Persian while she was there.

Her time spent in the region was the inspiration behind her first book, *Safar Nameh: Persian Pictures.* In 1897, she also published her English translations of *Poems from the Divan of Hafiz.*

Bell continued her travels in the Middle East, going everywhere from Palestine to Syria. She traveled through Arabia no less than six times over the next decade. On her journeys, Bell became skilled in Arabic, Persian, and other Ottoman languages. She also made tons of detailed maps of the regions and earned the trust and respect of the kings and tribal leaders everywhere she went. She took the time to get to know the locals and understand their customs.

Bell wrote about her experiences in the Middle East and was responsible for exposing the Western world to the Arabian desert for the first time with the publication in 1907 of *The Desert and the Sown.*

Bell's adventures in the early 1900s also included fascinating archaeological journeys. In 1909, she took a long trek down the Euphrates River and then worked on another archaeological project in Turkey with archaeologist Sir William Mitchell Ramsay. Together, they published *The Thousand and One Churches.*

Despite Bell's incredible intelligence and spirit for adventure, her love life was less successful. The first man she ever fell in love with was Henry Cadogan, who she met on a visit to Iran in 1892. Unfortunately, Cadogan suffered from bad gambling habits and had quite a bit of debt as a result, so Bell's father never approved.

Bell's next great love was British officer, Dick Doughty-Wylie, but he was married. His wife threatened suicide if he left her for Bell, but the conflict ended tragically with the death of Doughty-Wylie at the Battle of Gallipoli in 1915.

When World War I began, Bell requested a posting in the Middle East, but she was denied, so she started volunteering for the Red Cross. Shortly after, British Intelligence realized how useful her knowledge of the Middle East could be to them. They asked for Bell's help in getting their soldiers through the deserts, which she had so carefully mapped out over the previous decade.

From that point forward, Bell became crucial in shaping British policy in the Middle East. She also became the first woman officer to ever work for the British Military Intelligence.

During her posting with Britain in World War I, Bell worked closely with a colleague, T.E. Lawrence, in Cairo, where they were both assigned to Army Intelligence Headquarters in 1915. Lawrence and Bell worked diligently on forming alliances with Arab tribes, in an attempt to convince them to join the British against the Ottoman Empire.

On March 10, 1917, British troops took Baghdad, and they immediately called on Bell to assist them. She was named *"Oriental Secretary,"* and was given the assignment of analyzing the situation in the region. The British wanted her opinion on what was needed for future leadership, given her vast knowledge of the tribes. She spent almost a year writing a report for them.

By 1920, Bell was serving as a liaison between the incoming Arab government and British government officials. Bell's mediation between Shias, Sunnis, Kurds, the British, and numerous other groups, took an incredible amount of knowledge, sensitivity, social acumen, and political negotiation skills.

After playing a key role in determining the geographic and political structure for what was to become Iraq, in 1921 Bell was again called in to help ease Faisal bin Hussein, the First King of Iraq, into his role. She coached him on geography and local business and helped supervise cabinet appointees. The two became confidantes, and he later helped her found the Baghdad Archaeological Museum. Bell continued to remain an important part of the administration of Iraq throughout the 1920s.

In 1925, Bell finally returned to Britain for a brief time to deal with some family issues and her declining health. She didn't stay long, and when she returned to Baghdad, she developed pleurisy. As she was recovering, she learned that her younger brother, Hugh, had died of typhoid. Shortly after, on July 12, 1926, Bell was found dead from an overdose of sleeping pills. It is unknown whether it was suicide or an accidental overdose.

Bell's impact on the shaping of Iraq and enhancing Western knowledge of the Middle East during a pivotal time are the legacies of her productive and adventurous life.

GERTRUDE BELL: DID YOU KNOW?

1. In the early 1900s, Bell was lucky enough to take two entire trips around the world with her brother.

2. Bell had a passion for mountaineering, climbing peaks including the Meije and Les Ecrins in the Alps. She was also the first person, along with her two guides, to traverse an Alpine peak in the Bernese Oberland. The peak was named after her; its name is Gertrudspitze. As if that weren't enough, she once climbed the Alps in her underclothes because she said her skirt was too cumbersome.

3. One would assume that most educated and badass women would have been advocates for women's suffrage. Strangely enough, Gertrude was opposed to the suffragettes in England and served as honorary secretary of the British Women's Anti-Suffrage League.

4. Bell was a woman of many talents and stepped up to help people when they needed it. She ran a Wounded and Missing Enquiry Department for the Red Cross during World War I.

5. Bell was the first woman to ever travel alone in the Syrian desert.

6. Bell was often called the *"Queen of the Desert,"* and this became the title of a movie, starring Nicole Kidman, based on Bell's incredible life story.

7. Bell never married or had children.

8. Bell always had a passion for archaeology and later in life established the Baghdad Archaeological Museum, which is now called the Iraq Museum, in Baghdad. Bell personally brought in extensive collections to the museum. After Bell's death, a wing of the museum was named after her.

9. Bell almost lost her life on a mountaineering expedition. In 1902, Bell was climbing a mountain called the Finsteraarhorn, when a blizzard struck and made it nearly impossible for her and her guides to get back to the village at the bottom of the mountain. She spent over 50 hours on her rope until she was able to make it back. The incident didn't deter her from continuing to climb.

10. The people of Mesopotamia respected Bell so much that she was often referred to as *"khutan,"* meaning *"queen"* in Persian, and *"respected lady"* in Arabic.

CHAPTER 10:

HENRIETTA LACKS

Henrietta Lacks wasn't a doctor or a scientist, but she is still referred to as the *"mother of modern medicine,"* and her contributions to the medical field are insurmountable. Her *"immortal cells"* are still alive and helping scientists save uncountable lives today.

Henrietta Lacks entered this world on August 1, 1920, in Roanoke, Virginia. She was named Loretta but later changed her name to Henrietta. Sadly, her mother died when she was only four years old. Her father couldn't handle caring for 10 children on his own, so all of Henrietta's siblings were split up to live with different family members.

Henrietta was sent to live with her grandfather, Tommy, who resided in a four-room log cabin that the Lacks family called the *"home-house,"* which used to be slave quarters. Her grandfather was already the primary caregiver for another cousin, David Lacks, who the family called *"Day,"* and when Henrietta went to live in the cabin, they shared a room.

David and Henrietta's family was poor, but they did have the opportunity to attend school. David went to school until the 4th grade, and Henrietta stayed on until the 6th grade. When Henrietta wasn't in school, she spent her time in the tobacco fields with her cousin.

Selling tobacco was the family's primary source of income. The cousins would help pick and dry the tobacco, and their grandfather would take it into the city to auction to sell.

In 1935, when Henrietta was only 14 years old, she had a baby with David. Four years later, in 1939, they had a daughter, Elsie. A couple of years after they had Elsie, they got married. But life continued to be difficult and it was hard to make a living on the Lacks farm.

One of their cousins had moved to Maryland, near Baltimore, and was working for one of the Bethlehem Steel Corporation's plants, where he was making a decent living. He convinced David and Henrietta to join him there. David moved first to start saving up so he could bring Henrietta and the kids.

However, the cousin in Maryland got drafted and gave his savings to Day so he could bring Henrietta to live with him sooner.

In Maryland, they had three more children—two sons and a daughter. Their elder daughter, Elsie, suffered from epilepsy and was unable to speak. Her disability became so severe that, when they moved to Maryland, they had to admit her to a hospital called the *"Hospital for the Negro Insane."*

Unfortunately, after they moved to Maryland, Henrietta Lacks only had a short life ahead of her. She started experiencing sharp abdominal pain and bleeding, so she sought medical advice at Johns Hopkins Hospital, in Baltimore, Maryland. At the time, hospitals were still segregated, and Johns Hopkins was one of the few hospitals where African Americans could seek out treatment.

Her doctor, Howard Jones, diagnosed her with cervical cancer, and she underwent radiation. Unfortunately, Lacks didn't recover, and passed away on October 4, 1951, at the young age of 31.

However, Lacks' story did not end with her death at 31, and her impact on the medical field continues every single day. During her time at Johns Hopkins Hospital, unbeknownst to her family, doctors removed two cervical samples from Lacks' tumor. It is these two cells that were used to create the HeLa cell line, for which Lacks is known. Her cells have been vital to medical research ever since.

The incredibly unique thing about Lacks' cells is they were much more enduring than is typical. Researchers had been trying to grow cells in culture for years, but in every other attempt, the cells would die in just a few days. But not Henrietta Lacks' cells.

A researcher, Dr. George Otto Gey, recognized that the cells taken from Lacks were something special. Dr. Gey isolated and multiplied one of her cells, creating a cell line, which he named the HeLa cell line, after Henrietta Lacks. Her cells became the first *"immortal"* human cells and have been revolutionary to science.

The HeLa cells didn't just survive; they thrived and multiplied, so much so that labs have been using HeLa cells for research for over 65 years. Before the HeLa cells, researchers spent almost all their time just trying to keep cells alive. Having access to an endless supply of HeLa cells provided the time they needed to start making impactful discoveries in medical technology.

The first breakthrough using the HeLa strain was the creation of the polio vaccine. After the vaccine was invented, scientists began to recognize the demand for these incredible cells and cloned them in 1955.

The medical breakthroughs facilitated by HeLa cells didn't end with the development of the polio vaccine. Lacks' cells have been used in tens of thousands of scientific studies including ones that created drugs for leukemia, influenza, Parkinson's disease, HPV, and much more. Lacks' cells have even traveled to space to be used to study the impact on human cells of zero gravity in space.

Lacks' family didn't even learn that her cells were taken until the 1970s. Many ethical issues arose from the harvesting of Henrietta Lacks' cells without her permission. Not only were her cells harvested, they were also cloned, and sold by the billions, while her family remained so poor, they couldn't even afford health insurance.

Although they have tried, Lacks' family has had minimal success in getting rights to the HeLa strain. The only agreement they have come to so far was in 2013 with the National Institute of Health. This agreement granted the family the acknowledgment of Henrietta Lacks in scientific papers regarding the HeLa strain.

Although all scientists knew about the HeLa cell line, Lacks herself remained completely unknown to the world, despite her enormous contributions, until the release of a book in 2010 about her life, *The Immortal Life of Henrietta Lacks*. Subsequently, an HBO documentary was filmed starring Oprah Winfrey, which brought more awareness to the world about the contributions of Henrietta Lacks.

It's impossible to say how many lives have been saved thanks to the unknowing contribution of the cells of Henrietta Lacks. Though she died at the young age of 31, her legacy will live on forever.

HENRIETTA LACKS: DID YOU KNOW?

1. Rebecca Skloot, a science journalist, spent more than a decade researching the story of Henrietta Lacks and the HeLa cells, aiming to bring her contributions to light. She later published *The Immortal Life of Henrietta Lacks.*

2. The HPV vaccination was developed using the knowledge gained from Lacks' cells. This vaccine is credited with decreasing HPV in teenage girls by two-thirds.

3. In the 1960s, Lacks' cells were fused with mouse cells, and the first ever human-animal hybrid cells were created. These cells were crucial in gene mapping.

4. The HeLa cells are still being used for medical breakthroughs today. In 2019, microbiologists used the HeLa cells for research on the Zika virus. They found that the Zika virus can't multiply in HeLa cells, which could very soon result in a treatment or vaccine for Zika, a serious public health risk, particularly to pregnant women.

5. In 2018, Johns Hopkins University announced that it would be constructing and naming a building after Henrietta Lacks to honor her legacy. The expected completion date of the building is 2022.

6. HBO launched a multi-media art exhibit called *"The HeLa Project"* to celebrate Lacks, featuring an original portrait by artist Kadir Nelson, an original poem by Saul

Williams, and a song by recording artist Jazmine Sullivan. The exhibit toured through numerous United States cities, including New York City and Atlanta. The portrait of Lacks now hangs in the National Portrait Gallery at the Smithsonian.

7. HeLa cells are so prevalent that you can order them over the phone from multiple 1-800 numbers. The cells are also available online from numerous websites.

8. Some scientists believe that the HeLa cells are a whole new species. Dr. Leigh Van Valen wrote a paper that was published in 1991, stating that he thinks the HeLa cells should be acknowledged as a new life form. Other researchers disagree.

9. IVF (in vitro fertilization) is one of the most common types of assisted reproductive technologies available to couples who are having trouble getting pregnant. IVF is just another advancement we can thank Lacks for. Using HeLa cells, scientists were able to learn how to isolate one cell and keep it alive, which is the basis of IVF. IVF has been groundbreaking in helping women overcome fertility issues, and it's estimated that over half a million babies are born each year through IVF.

10. If you combined all the HeLa cells in existence, they could circle the equator three times and would weigh more than 100 Empire State Buildings.

CHAPTER 11:

THE MIRABAL SISTERS

Sometimes revolutionaries come from the most unlikely of places. Four Dominican sisters were courageous enough to stand up to a brutal dictator in the Dominican Republic, and in death became martyrs for their cause. Their story is known to most Dominicans, but it's relatively unknown to the rest of the world.

The four Mirabal sisters—Patria, Minerva, María Teresa, and Dedé—were the children of a middle class, conservative family of landowners in a rural area of the Dominican Republic in the Salcedo Province. Their father, Enrique Mirabal Fernández, was strict and kept the sisters in a sheltered environment. Their mother, Mercedes Reyes Camilo, could barely read or write but wanted her daughters to get an education.

The oldest sister, Patria Mercedes Mirabal Reyes, was born on February 27, 1924. At the age of 14, her parents sent her to receive a good education at a Catholic boarding school called Colegio Inmaculada Concepción in La Vega. When she was 17, Patria left school and married a farmer, Pedro Gonzalez, and they had two children.

The second sister, Bélgica Adela Mirabal Reyes (known as Dedé), was born on March 1, 1925. She did not go on to further education; instead, she helped run the family business and became a homemaker. She was less involved in her three sisters' political efforts, although she played a major part in ensuring their legacy lives on.

The third sister, María Argentina Minerva Mirabal Reyes (known as Minerva), was born on March 12, 1926. When she was 12, she followed in her eldest sister's footsteps to boarding school. After secondary school, she furthered her education at the University of Santo Domingo. Following her college graduation, she decided to attend graduate school and pursue a law degree.

The youngest sister was Antonia María Teresa Mirabal Reyes (known as María Teresa). She was born on October 15, 1935. In 1954, she graduated from the Liceo de San Francisco de

Macorís and then pursued a degree in mathematics at the University of Santo Domingo. After she completed her degree, María Teresa married Leandro Guzmán.

One thing that the sisters had in common was they all developed strong social consciences while living during a turbulent time in the Dominican Republic. They lived under the cruel dictator Rafael Leónidas Trujillo Molina, who ruled the country for almost three decades. His despotic regime began in 1930, shortly after the United States ended its occupation of the Dominican Republic and approved the leadership of Trujillo, even though he won the presidency through a compromised election.

Trujillo's rule was characterized by murder, bribery, disappearances, unwanted sexual advances toward women, and numerous other crimes against humanity. Life under the horrific dictatorship of Rafael Trujillo was a time of fear for Dominicans. Anyone who dared to criticize him disappeared. Neighbors—and even family members—turned on each other, and turned people in. Residents lived in constant fear of Trujillo's secret police pulling up to their home in their distinctive black Volkswagens.

Unfortunately, at the young age of 22, one of the Mirabal sisters, Minerva, learned first-hand what it was like for women who were the victims of Trujillo's unwanted sexual advances. When she was in law school, she turned down sexual advances from Trujillo. As a result, she was kicked out of law school and put in jail. She spent three years under house arrest in her parents' home, where she passed the time writing poetry about the suffering people were being forced to endure in her beloved country.

Eventually, Minerva was able to return to finish her studies and graduated with honors at the National Autonomous University of the Dominican Republic. She met her husband, Manolo Tavárez Justo, at the university and he later became a great supporter of hers in the fight against Trujillo.

The Mirabal sisters were strong, educated, and outspoken. They didn't want to live under Trujillo's corrupt regime and began to get involved in the revolution. Their decision to participate in the revolution was rare; in Hispanic culture in the Dominican Republic at that time it was common for women to take a more passive role, and people lived in such fear of Trujillo.

The most radical of the sisters, and the first to get involved in the cause, was Minerva. Her sisters joined her shortly after, as they continued to witness the brutality of his regime. Regardless, Minerva was constantly singled out and Trujillo often gave direct orders for her arrest and harassment.

Though numerous factors contributed to the radicalization of the Mirabal sisters, the success of the Cuban revolution in 1959 played a prominent role in inciting political activity in many Dominicans, including the sisters. Despite the obvious danger in getting involved, three of the Mirabal sisters— Patria, Minerva, and María Teresa—and their husbands became strong political leaders.

The sisters helped found the underground movement called the *"14th of June Movement,"* which was named after a massacre of revolutionaries that one of the sisters witnessed while she was on a spiritual retreat in the mountains of the Dominican Republic. The movement educated people by handing out pamphlets highlighting the lives of Trujillo's victims and the disturbing details of his cruel dictatorship. The Mirabal sisters and their husbands continued to be thrown in jail for their political activities, but they never let their fear or incarcerations stop them.

One night, on November 25, 1960, Patria, Minerva, and María Teresa were on their way home after visiting their husbands, who had been imprisoned at Puerto Plata prison, when they were attacked by soldiers. The three sisters, along with their driver, were strangled and brutally clubbed to death. The assailants then put their bodies back in their Jeep and rolled it over a cliff to make it look like an accident and cover up the bodies.

The newspapers described the incident as a *"car accident,"* but the public didn't buy it. They knew it was no accident; it was clear the Mirabal sisters were assassinated because of their involvement in the fight against the dictatorship of Rafael Trujillo. The news of what happened to the sisters spread like wildfire across the Dominican Republic.

The women became martyrs, and historians today attribute the assassination of the Mirabal sisters as a true turning point in the brutal dictatorship of Rafael Trujillo. Their actions leading up to their death, and how he treated these women — who were wives and mothers—eventually led to Trujillo's demise.

Following her three sisters' assassinations, the only remaining sister, Dedé, became a mother to the six nieces and nephews left behind, in addition to her own three children.

Dedé founded the Mirabal Museo, the second home of the Mirabal families, to keep the memories of her three sisters alive. For the remainder of her life, she would personally greet many of the visitors to the museum. Her family continues to carry on the tradition at the museum today. On November 25th, 2000, the 40th anniversary of the Mirabal sisters' assassination, their remains were moved to the museum grounds where they can rest peacefully together.

Everyone in the Dominican Republic knows the story of the Mirabal sisters and they have become heroines. In nearly every Dominican town you can find schools, streets, and commemorative markers named after the Mirabal sisters.

Internationally, the three women have become symbols of women and human rights. In 1999, The United States General Assembly designated November 25, the day the Mirabal sisters were killed in 1960, as the International Day for Elimination of Violence Against Women. The date is also the beginning of the 16 Days of Activism Against Gender Violence, which ends on December 10, Human Rights Day.

THE MIRABAL SISTERS:
DID YOU KNOW?

1. The Mirabal sisters were known as *"Las Mariposas,"* which translates to *"The Butterflies."* The Mirabal sisters chose the butterfly as the symbol of their fight for freedom and independence for their country.

2. The second born of the four sisters, Dedé, never fully participated with the others in their opposition of Trujillo, and as a result, she lived a long and full life. She died peacefully in 2014 at the age of 88. She was the inspiration behind the book about the Mirabal sisters, *In the Time of Butterflies,* an award-winning novel written by Julia Alvarez. The book was made into a movie in 2001 starring Salma Hayek and Edward James Olmos.

3. The Mirabal sisters were named in *TIME*'s list of the *"100 Women of the Year,"* recognizing the most influential women of the last century.

4. In 1935, Trujillo built a 137-foot obelisk to commemorate his renaming of the capital city of Santo Domingo to Ciudad Trujillo. It has now been covered with murals that honor the Mirabal sisters.

5. *"The Butterflies"* are featured on the 200 Dominican pesos bill. The Dominican Republic has also issued a stamp to commemorate the sisters.

6. In 2009, a documentary film about the Mirabal sisters was released by the Chilean filmmaker, Cecilia Domeyko. *Code Name: Butterflies* was the first documentary about the heroines.

7. In 2010, Michelle Rodriguez, a Dominican actress, co-produced and starred in Trópico de Sangre, a movie about the Mirabal sisters. The film made its debut in the United States at the New York International Latino Film Festival, where it was well-received.

8. Before commencing their activism, the Mirabal family was invited to a party at Trujillo's mansion. The sisters decided to leave the party early, and Trujillo was offended, feeling that the women had disrespected him. As a result of this simple act, he had the entire family thrown in prison.

9. Many feared for the Mirabal sisters' lives, particularly Minerva's, because she was targeted most often. When people would express their fear for Minerva, she would say, *"If they kill me, I'll reach my arms out from the tomb and I'll be stronger."* Little did she know at the time that she would become a martyr.

10. In 2007, the Salcedo Province where the Mirabal sisters grew up was renamed the Hermanas Mirabal Province.

CHAPTER 12:

MALALA YOUSAFZAI

There are badass women from around the world, from all periods, but few fearless leaders in history emerged as young as Malala Yousafzai, a champion of human rights and education for all.

Malala was born on July 12, 1997, in Mingora, Pakistan, which is now known as Khyber Pakhtunkhwa Province of Pakistan. She lived with her mother, father, and two brothers in their home in the Swat Valley, a beautiful place that she loved.

From a young age, Malala loved school. Her father, to whom she was always remarkably close, was the founder of the Khushal Girls High School and College in the city of Mingora, which provided a wonderful education to girls of all ages. Her father says that, as a toddler, Malala would wander around the classrooms and pretend to teach people.

Some people just have a thirst for learning, and Malala is one of those people. She loved school, devoured her books, and was frequently top of her class at the Khushal School. Malala had a pretty regular childhood, spending her time going to school, fighting with her younger brothers, playing cricket in the alley, and reading the *Twilight* novels, expressing in her memoir that she was not an Edward fan.

Unfortunately, Malala came of age during a difficult time for the people of Pakistan, when the Taliban started to gain control. In 2007, when Malala was just 10 years old, the Taliban started taking over and implemented strict Islamic law.

Malala recalls the first scary signs of the Taliban taking over her beloved Swat Valley. She heard a militant, nicknamed *"Radio Mullah,"* starting to speak about the need for imposing strict Islamic law. He began by speaking of banning things like watching television, deeming it too Western.

The broadcast then proceeded to state that women should not go out in public, and that included girls going to school. The Taliban made the banning of education for girls a priority in their campaign of terror. By 2008, they had destroyed an estimated 400 schools.

Malala's father was an activist and an educator and spoke out against the Taliban frequently. Soon Malala began to speak out as well. The amazing thing about Malala is the courage she displayed at an incredibly young age. In September 2008, at the age of 11, Malala gave her first speech, *"How Dare the Taliban Take Away My Basic Right to Education?"*

Her speech was broadcast on Pakistani TV and aired throughout the nation. Shortly after her speech, the Taliban officially shut down all girls' schools in the Swat Valley.

Malala wanted to go to school and she wasn't afraid to speak out against the Taliban. When the British Broadcasting Company (BBC) approached her father to see if he had any girls in his school who would be willing to blog anonymously about life under the Taliban and the ban against girls' education, Malala volunteered. She was still 11 years old.

Under the pseudonym *"Gul Makai,"* Malala wrote more than 35 blog entries about her fears, her desire to go to school, and life in general under Taliban rule.

In 2009, Malala and her entire family were displaced. They had to leave their beloved Swat Valley and make a long, treacherous journey to stay with their relatives until it was safe to return.

Despite the apparent danger, Malala did not stop speaking out. In 2009, she worked with *New York Times* reporter Adam Ellick to make two documentaries; *Class Dismissed,* about the school's shut down, and *A Schoolgirl's Odyssey.* The *New York Times* released both films on their website, and they were shown around the world.

Malala continued to appear on local and international media, and in December 2009 her identity as the BBC's blogger became known. She began to be recognized internationally for her activism against the Taliban. In 2011, Malala was nominated by Desmond Tutu for the International Children's Peace Prize. That same year, she became the first person to receive Pakistan's National Youth Peace Prize, which they have since renamed the National Malala Peace Prize.

Malala became an enemy of the Taliban and a target of their violence. On her bus ride home from school on October 9, 2012, there was an assassination attempt on Malala's life. She was shot in the head by the Taliban, and it's a miracle she survived. Two other girls were injured in the attack. Malala was just 15 years old at the time of the attack.

After being treated in Pakistan, Malala was put in a medically induced coma and airlifted to the Queen Elizabeth Hospital in Birmingham, England. Her family was unable to go with her, so she went alone. Her parents made a doctor her legal guardian for the journey.

When Malala first awoke, she was confused, and the doctors didn't want to tell her what had happened. They told her that her parents would be there soon, and they would explain. Finally, the doctor explained that Malala had been shot in the head by the Taliban.

While many teenagers would have been concerned with their looks, Malala was just grateful to be alive. She states in her book that, when they arrived in England, her parents seemed more disturbed by her looks than she did.

Malala had to have multiple surgeries, including a repair of a facial nerve because the entire left side of her face was paralyzed. Thankfully, she suffered no brain damage from her injuries. After a long recovery, she was finally able to return to school in March 2013 in Birmingham, England.

It was too dangerous for Malala and her family to return to Pakistan, so they made a new life for themselves in England. Malala admits in her book that it was difficult for them, and she frequently missed the sights and smells of her beautiful Swat Valley. But they adjusted, and it became home.

Being shot in the head by the Taliban could not stop Malala. Just nine months after being shot, she appeared in front of the United Nations on her 16th birthday and gave a speech in which she advocated for education and women's rights.

July 12, Malala's birthday, was designated as *"World Malala Day"* by the United Nations on Malala's 16th birthday. Every July 12, the world celebrates women's and children's rights.

In 2013, Malala released her memoir, *I am Malala: The Girl Who Stood Up for Education and Was Shot by the Taliban,* which she co-authored with Christina Lamb, a correspondent for *The Sunday Times.*

Shortly after her speech to the U. N., the European Parliament presented Malala with the Sakharov Prize for Freedom of Thought, a huge honor. Then, at the age of 17, Malala became the youngest person to ever be awarded the Nobel Peace Prize. She became a Nobel Prize laureate in 2014, sharing the prize with children's rights activist, Kailash Satyarthi.

After she won the Nobel Prize, Malala continued to use her newly elevated public profile to draw attention to human rights issues around the world. Utilizing the Malala Fund, she was able to open a girls' school for refugees from the Syrian Civil War in Lebanon. The school opened in July 2015. Malala wrote another book about her work with refugees in 2019 called *We Are Displaced: My Journey and Stories from Refugee Girls Around the World.*

The world is lucky to have Malala, who continues to fight every day for us all.

MALALA YOUSAFZAI: DID YOU KNOW?

1. Malala is true to her namesake, Malalai of Maiwand, a poet and warrior. Malalai was a heroine in the Second Anglo-Afghan War, a rebellion against the British that took place from 1878 until 1880. She was a true Pashtun warrior who fought against colonialism.

2. In 2013, Malala was named as one of *Time Magazine*'s most influential people of the year.

3. When Malala first met President Barack Obama and First Lady Michelle Obama, she wasn't afraid to speak her mind. She asked the president to stop the drone strikes in Pakistan because they were killing innocent people. Malala also expressed that if the United States spent as much money on education as it did on weapons and war, the world would be a better place.

4. Malala loved watching the American tv show *Ugly Betty* when she lived in Pakistan. When she finally got the opportunity to go to New York City, she felt right at home because she had spent so much time watching the show.

5. When she was a young teenager, one of Malala's greatest wishes was to grow another inch. She would pray to Allah every night and ask him to make her grow taller.

6. Despite her dedication to peace around the world, Malala still fought with her younger brothers, Atal and Khushal.

When she received the Nobel Peace Prize she stated, *"I am pretty certain that I am also the first recipient of the Nobel Peace Prize who still fights with her younger brothers."*

7. In 2015, NASA named an asteroid after Malala. The asteroid's formal designation is 316201 Malala.

8. A documentary was filmed about Malala's family, *He Named Me Malala.* It was released in October 2015.

9. Malala became the youngest person to win the Liberty Medal in 2014, awarded by the National Constitution Center in Philadelphia, which recognizes those fighting for people's freedom around the world.

10. Malala wrote a picture book inspired by her childhood, titled *Malala's Magic Pencil,* published in 2017. It encourages children to find magic everywhere.

CHAPTER 13:

MARIE CURIE

Badass women are those who the world wouldn't be the same without. They are people that use their brains to contribute to the world and try to make it a better place. Marie Curie's contributions to the world of science are insurmountable. As the first person to win the Nobel Prize twice, she was a special person who graced history with her genius.

Marie Curie was born Maria Salomea Skłodowska on November 7, 1867, in Warsaw, Poland. She was the youngest of a family of five, with siblings Zosia, Józio, Bronya, and Hela. The odds were against Maria in many ways, beginning early on in life. She never had it easy. Both of her parents were teachers, and not financially well-off. They took in boarders so they could pay for their home, and Maria slept on the family couch.

In addition to the family's difficult financial situation, it was a tough time to live in Poland. Warsaw was under Russian rule, and they attempted to forbid the Polish from embracing their heritage, even banning Polish from being spoken.

Regardless, Maria attended school and she quickly proved to be the smartest child in her class. But hardships continued to plague her. Her older sister caught typhus from one of their boarders and died when Maria was only eight years old. A little more than two years later her mother, Bronisława, died of tuberculosis.

Maria continued to do well in school, despite her sadness. She completed her high school education in 1883 at the age of 15 and finished first in her class in every subject.

Following her high school graduation, Maria became extremely ill and collapsed. Her doctors at the time diagnosed her with *"fatigue"* and *"nervousness."* In today's world, she might have been diagnosed with depression. Her father insisted that she take a much-needed break in the countryside with her cousins. There, she lived a carefree life, which she hadn't been able to do much during a childhood filled with hardship.

When she returned, Maria knew she wanted to continue her education and go on to study at university. However, the Russian government had made it illegal for any Polish woman to attend the University of Warsaw. Unwilling to give up on her education, she began attending an illegal *"floating university"* with her sister, Bronya.

The illegal school held classes at night in different locations every time, to avoid detection from the authorities. The *"floating university"* also helped to aid Polish liberation, and Maria received a solid introduction to the progressive thinking of the time. She was interested in science and learned a little, but she knew it couldn't come close to what she could be learning from a regular university curriculum.

Maria and her sister Bronya came up with an idea. They would pool their finances so that they could both move to France and attend the University of Paris. As the youngest, Maria would work to support her sister, then Bronya would help support Maria.

Working as a governess, Maria was able to make good money to support her sister. All was going well until she fell in love with the family's oldest son, Kazimierz Żorawski. He wanted to marry Maria, and his parents were not pleased. They respected the wishes of the parents and broke off their engagement, but Maria remained romantically involved with him for a few years.

During her time as a governess, Maria spent as much time studying as she could. She read a lot on her own, took a math class from her father, and took chemistry lessons from a chemist who worked in her employer's beet-sugar factory.

Finally, after their father started earning more money and supplemented the two sisters' income, Maria was able to join her sister. In 1891, at the age of 24, she set off to meet Bronya and begin her studies at the University of Paris.

When she moved to Paris, Maria became Marie. Her name change was one of many changes she encountered in France. Marie found that she was behind her fellow students. Not being fluent in French, understanding the lessons was a challenge.

She was also extremely poor, to the point that she was malnourished. Marie would go to class during the day and tutor at night. She survived on little but tea and buttered bread and would faint from hunger. Regardless of her disadvantages, she didn't let them hold her back. She graduated first in her master's degree courses in physics in 1893.

Following her physics degree courses, she enrolled in a math program. It was around this time that she found herself in need of a lab, and was introduced to Pierre Curie, who was already famous for his groundbreaking research on magnetism. Pierre Curie fell for Marie's love and passion for science, which he also shared. He once gave her an autographed copy of one of his physics papers as a token of affection.

When Marie completed her degree in mathematics, she returned to Poland, unsure if she would return to France. When she decided to return, Pierre was a part of the reason.

He sent her numerous love letters trying to convince her to return to Paris and pursue her doctorate.

The two married in a non-religious and non-traditional ceremony. Curie wore a dark blue suit that she could wear again, as she was a practical woman. Although they didn't have a traditional wedding, they did decide to embark on a honeymoon. They toured France on bicycles that were given to them as wedding gifts.

The rest of their union was far from typical. They went on to make some of science's most groundbreaking discoveries together, including the discovery of two new elements: polonium in the summer of 1898, and radium shortly after.

In 1897, Curie became a mother to a daughter, Irene. Despite these new responsibilities, Marie and Pierre never considered putting her science career on hold. Pierre's father watched Irene, while Curie continued to work on her research and start working towards her doctorate in science.

Once Curie discovered radioactivity, Pierre put aside his work, and the two became a brilliant scientific duo. Curie spent the early 1900s trying to obtain pure radium in a metallic state, which she eventually achieved.

1903 and 1904 were happy and successful years for the Curies. Marie earned her doctorate in science in June 1903 and was awarded the Davy Medal of the Royal Society, along with her husband. That same year, the Curies received the Nobel Prize for Physics for their discovery of radioactivity. And in 1904 they welcomed their second daughter, Ève, into the world.

Sadly, just a couple of years after winning the Nobel Prize, Marie suffered the blow of the tragic death of her husband and scientific partner, Pierre. On April 19, 1906, Pierre was crossing a busy street in Paris, and he slipped and fell under a horse-drawn cart, and one of the wheels ran him over.

Faced with tragedy, Marie didn't quit; she continued their scientific research. She even took over the vacant position left in the wake of her husband's death, becoming the first woman to ever teach in the Sorbonne. In 1911, Curie won the Nobel Prize for Chemistry, for her work in successfully isolating pure radium.

At the onset of World War I, Curie developed a great passion to help the war effort. When France needed gold, she even offered them her Nobel Prizes to melt down. They refused to take them, so she started using all the prize money she won to purchase war bonds. Her efforts to help in the war didn't stop with her fundraising efforts.

The Curies' research was instrumental in the development of x-rays in surgery. During World War I, Marie realized that x-rays could make a big difference in the lives of soldiers. She requested that the government appoint her as the director of the Red Cross Radiology Service, and solicited donations from her wealthy friends to fund a mobile x-ray machine that could be installed in cars, along with generators, to act as ambulances.

After her invention proved that it could save lives, Curie made 20 additional vehicles to aid in the war efforts, and all of them were operated by a team of women. The machines were called *"petite Curies."*

Curie went on to install 200 more machines at field hospitals. She saved an estimated one million lives with these efforts. Not only did Curie invent and install the machines, she even drove and operated the portable x-ray vehicle herself to treat soldiers on the front lines at the Battle of Marne.

Following World War I, Curie spent some time traveling and giving lectures, speaking in many countries including Brazil, Spain, Belgium, and Czechoslovakia. In 1921, she went to the United States and President Warren G. Harding presented her with one gram of radium, on behalf of the women of the United States of America (she needed the radium for her ongoing research).

Later in her life, Curie worked towards building foundations and laboratories to continue her life's work. The Curie Foundation was created in Paris, and in 1932 the Radium Institute in Warsaw was established with Curie's sister, Bronya, as its director. Curie worked extremely hard to create a radioactivity laboratory in her home city. In 1929, President Hoover even presented her with $50,000 to buy radium to use in the lab in Warsaw.

Curie worked with radium for her whole career and spent a great deal of time learning about its potential to make advances in the medical field. Ironically, it was her work with radioactivity that ended up killing her. Curie died on July 4, 1934, at the age of 66, from aplastic anemia from her exposure to radiation.

MARIE CURIE: DID YOU KNOW?

1. Marie Curie is the only person to ever receive two Nobel Prizes in two separate sciences.

2. Curie's daughter, Irene, and Irene's husband, Frédéric Joliot-Curie, won the Nobel Prize for chemistry in 1935 for their discovery of artificial radioactivity. Marie's son-in-law, Henry Labouisse, who married their youngest daughter, Ève, won a Nobel Prize for Peace on behalf of UNICEF, where he worked as the Executive Director. Collectively, the Curie family has now won five Nobel Prizes.

3. Curie was the first woman to ever receive a Ph.D. from a French university.

4. Curie was exposed to a great deal of radium, which significantly impacted her health. It also affected her notebooks, which are still radioactive after over a century. It is estimated that they will be radioactive for another 1500 years and are now stored in lead-lined boxes.

5. After they discovered radium, Marie and her husband refused to reap financial benefits from their discovery. They did not patent it, so they did not profit from the production of radium. Instead, they shared the information with fellow researchers and even distributed the information on how to produce it to industrial representatives who were interested in its production.

Ironically, by the 1920s, the price of radium skyrocketed so high that a gram of the new element discovered by the Curies reached an average of $100,000; Curie couldn't even afford to purchase it to work on her research.

6. In 1995, Curie became the first woman to receive the honor of having her ashes enshrined in the Panthéon in Paris for her life achievements.

7. Albert Einstein and Marie Curie became friends at a conference in Belgium in 1911. During one of the darkest times of her life, Curie received a kind letter from Einstein, expressing his admiration for her work, and offered heartfelt advice on handling a recent fabricated scandal she was facing in the press.

8. Curie and her husband didn't have access to a regular lab. They discovered radium and polonium in a shed, where they conducted the majority of their research and experiments.

9. Curie never forgot her Polish roots. When her children were little, she hired tutors to make sure her daughters learned Polish when they were growing up. She even named the element she discovered, Polonium, after her home country.

10. Curie once applied for a position at the Polish University of Krakow, but she was denied it due to her gender.

CHAPTER 14:

SOJOURNER TRUTH

Most people know Sojourner Truth as a strong, Black woman who delivered her famous speech, *"Ain't I a Woman?"* But there is so much more that makes her inspirational. She was the first Black woman to win a lawsuit against a White man in the United States. Following slavery, she didn't fall apart; she reinvented herself and thrived. Truth became the only enslaved woman to lead a public, oratory life.

Sojourner Truth was born in the late 1790s; most historians

agree on the year 1797, but no one tracked this information when she was born. She was born a slave, and like most slaves, she didn't know her exact birthday. At birth, she was named Isabella Baumfree by her parents.

Isabella's parents, James and Elizabeth, were the slaves of Colonel Johannes Hardenbergh, a Revolutionary War colonel. James was captured in Ghana and taken to America, while Elizabeth was the daughter of two slaves from Guinea. Beyond that, there isn't much information about Sojourner Truth's genealogy, as is the case with most slaves.

Isabella was born the youngest of 10 or 12 brothers and sisters, but she only ever knew one of her siblings, as they were sold before she was born. It was common for slave children to be sold and taken away from their parents, a heartbreak that Isabella's parents never got over.

Isabella was born in Swartekill, New York. Most people now associate slavery in the United States with the South, but there were once thousands of slaves in New York. She was born in a Dutch community, only about 90 miles from New York City. Isabella grew up speaking Dutch as her first language, which would soon become a problem.

When Isabella was only nine years old, she was sold at an auction for the price of $100. The farmer she was sold to, John Neely, was a violent man, and she frequently faced whippings. He was frustrated that she didn't follow instructions, but his household spoke English, and her first language was Dutch.

She was sold twice more before she ended up with the family

with whom she spent the longest part of her enslaved life, the Dumonts. Isabella worked completing household tasks for the mistress, and fieldwork tasks for John Dumont. She suffered both physical and sexual abuse as a slave with the Dumonts, but she stayed in touch with them throughout life.

When she was a young teenager, Isabella fell in love with a man named Robert, who was a slave at another farm nearby. It is believed that her first daughter, Diana, was Robert's child. However, Robert's master forbid the relationship because any children the couple had would become the property of John Dumont, not himself. Robert was beaten nearly to death, and the two ended their relationship.

John Dumont instructed Isabella to marry one of his slaves, Thomas, who was older than her. The two had three children: a son named Peter, and two daughters, Elizabeth and Sophia. In her later writings, Truth didn't comment much on her relationship with Thomas. It was not a marriage born out of love, but one dictated by their master.

A landmark moment arrived for Isabella when the state of New York passed legislation that would free all slaves. John Dumont had promised Isabella that he would free her in the year 1826, but he took back his promise when she became injured. Although the state of New York planned to emancipate all slaves in the state on July 4, 1827, Isabella didn't want to wait for her freedom. She escaped with her infant daughter, Sophia.

Isabella had to make the heart-wrenching decision to leave

her husband and other children behind, including her five-year-old son Peter. She left with just a handkerchief full of food, but she didn't travel far. She traveled to a friend about five miles away, who directed her to a family who was against slavery, the Van Wagenens. They kindly let her stay with them. When John Dumont showed up at the family's home to bring her back, they paid him $20 for Sojourner and $5 for baby Sophia to buy their freedom. She spent a peaceful and kind year with the family following her escape.

Shortly after her escape, Isabella found out that her son, Peter, had been sold to a man in Alabama. After the New York Anti-Slavery Law was passed, it was illegal to sell a slave across state lines in New York. Isabella decided to file a lawsuit to get her son back. She won the case and got custody of Peter. She became the first Black woman to sue a White man in court in the United States and win.

It didn't become easy for Isabella once she was free; she had to work hard. She moved to New York City and worked for numerous families as a housekeeper. One of the people she worked for was a minister, and throughout the 1830s, Isabella became heavily involved in the religious community. She started becoming the charismatic speaker that she's known as today.

In 1843, Isabella renamed herself. She believed that she was called to speak the truth and thus renamed herself *"Sojourner Truth."* In 1844, Truth became a member of an active abolitionist organization called the Northampton Association of Education and Industry. It was during this time that she met important abolitionists, such as Frederick Douglass. She launched what would become her lifetime career as an equal rights activist, speaking out for women and slaves.

Truth never learned to read or write, but she didn't let that stop her from leaving a legacy behind in writing. She dictated the story of her life as a slave and her transformation into an abolitionist and feminist. Her dictated words and songs were written down by Olive Gilbert. Truth's autobiography, *The Narrative of Sojourner Truth,* was published in 1850. The following year, she embarked on a tour to promote her book and continue speaking out for the causes in which she believed.

Truth gave her famous speech, *"Ain't I a Woman?"*, in 1851 at the Ohio Women's Rights Convention, which she attended to speak out about equal rights for Black women. She met women's rights leaders such as Elizabeth Cady Stanton and Susan B. Anthony. Her famous speech at the convention was just one of many engaging, provocative speeches she made throughout her lifetime as an orator.

During the American Civil War, Truth became much more political, a shift that would continue throughout her life. She was a member of the National Freedman's Relief Association in Washington, D.C., where she worked to get donations of food, clothes, and other essential supplies to Black refugees from the South. She also worked to recruit Black soldiers to fight for the Union Army in the war. Aside from the war cause, Truth took it upon herself to protest segregation by courageously riding in Whites-only streetcars.

Later in life, Truth moved to Battle Creek, Michigan, where her daughters resided. However, she never stopped speaking publicly about her passion for women's suffrage and her disdain for discrimination and segregation. She also frequently addressed the fact that many male civil rights leaders thought that equal rights for Black men should be put ahead of equal rights for Black women.

Truth passed away on November 26, 1883, at the age of 86. Her tombstone reads, *"Is God Dead,"* a question she once asked someone when reminding them to have faith.

SOJOURNER TRUTH: DID YOU KNOW?

1. Truth was invited to the White House by Abraham Lincoln in 1864. During her visit, she told Lincoln the story of her life as a slave. Lincoln showed her a bible given to him by Black residents from Baltimore.

2. The United States has chosen Truth to appear on the $10 Bill, but as of 2020, the exact release date is unclear.

3. When she was living in New York City, in 1834, Truth was charged with murdering Elijah Pierson, a Christian Evangelist who she worked for as a housekeeper. Truth, along with a man by the name of Robert Matthews, was accused of stealing from Pierson and poisoning him. The two went on trial and were both acquitted.

4. NASA named the Mars Rover *"Sojourner"* after Truth.

5. A streetcar conductor tried to force Truth out of his vehicle in 1865, and in the process, he dislocated her arm. Truth sued him, and the conductor lost his job. Additionally, she forced the streetcar company to finally start enforcing Washington D.C.'s desegregation laws.

6. Truth was one of the first people in the United States to use photography to earn a living. Truth sold photographs at her lectures and through the mail to support herself. Called *"carte de visite,"* these small prints mounted on cards were used to raise funds and market Truth, a

marketing masterstroke. She even took it a step further and copyrighted her image. The money she made funded her speaking tours across the country.

7. Truth could be found working tirelessly at the Freedmen's Village of Washington D.C., where she taught sewing, knitting, and cooking to emancipated field slaves so they could learn to financially support themselves.

8. Truth's son Peter, who she went to court to save, got a job on a whaling ship in 1839. She received a few letters from him, but when the ship returned in 1842, Peter wasn't on it, and she never heard from him again.

9. Released in 2018, *Truth* is an Emmy Award-winning animated short film directed by Kyle Portbury that's based on Sojourner Truth's speech, *"Ain't I a Woman?"* It was filmed as the first episode in a film series titled, *"True Heroes."*

10. In 2014, Truth was listed in the *Smithsonian* magazine's *"100 Most Significant Americans of All Time."*

CHAPTER 15:

BILLIE JEAN KING

Billie Jean King was born Billie Jean Moffitt on November 22, 1943, in Long Beach, California. Her father, Bill, was a firefighter, and her mother, Betty, stayed at home to take care of the family. She came from a family of athletes; her father once tried out for the NBA, and Betty was a talented swimmer. She has one sibling, Randy, who became a Major League Baseball pitcher for the San Francisco Giants, Houston Astros, and the Toronto Blue Jays.

Surprisingly, Billie Jean's first sport was not tennis. She started with basketball and then moved onto softball. She excelled in other sports, and when she was just 10 years old, her softball team won the city championship.

It wasn't until 5th grade that Billie Jean's father suggested she give tennis a try. She began playing with her friend, Susan Williams, who took her to a country club. Billie Jean says she knew immediately that she wanted to play tennis for the rest of her life. She saved up to purchase a racquet, which she began playing with at Long Beach's public tennis courts.

Sadly, in the 1950s, discrimination against women in sports was prevalent. Billie Jean was banned from participating in a junior tennis tournament at the Los Angeles Tennis Club in 1955 because she was wearing tennis shorts instead of the traditional tennis dress worn by women athletes.

People began to notice the impressive talents of Billie Jean when she won a Southern California championship in 1958. The following year, she went pro under the coaching of Alice Marble, a former women's tennis pro player.

Billie Jean didn't let tennis stop her from going to college. She attended California State University in Los Angeles. During her time there, she became a tennis coach and continued to compete in tournaments.

In 1965, Billie Jean married a law student, Larry King. The two became best friends and spent many happy years together. They never had any children.

Billie Jean King entered the international tennis stage in 1961, when she and Karen Hantze Susman became the youngest pair to win the women's doubles title at Wimbledon. After winning this title, King intensified her training. In 1966, she won her first singles championship at Wimbledon and was ranked the number one women's tennis player in the world, a title which she held for five years.

King didn't stop pushing herself and winning year after year. Over the next 18 years, she won 20 Wimbledon titles, 13 United States titles, four French titles, and two Australian titles, equaling 39 Grand Slam titles in total. No one could touch her, and she could have stopped there. Surely, being an international star was enough?

But winning wasn't enough for Billie Jean King, because she wanted equality, not just for herself, but for all women. In the 1970s in the United States, female tennis champions were receiving less prize money than male tennis champions in the same competitions. King was making a lot of money—more money than any other woman had won before—but it still wasn't equal, and that was unacceptable to her.

In 1971, King broke another record, becoming the first woman athlete to ever earn over $100,000 in prize money. Yet, at her next U.S. open competition in 1971, she received $15,000 less than the men's champion.

King used her fame and talent as leverage to fight for equality for women. She formed the Women's Tennis Association (WTA) and was its first acting president. In her new role, she rallied for the cause of equal prize money for men and women in the U.S. Open, a fight that was eventually won. The U.S. Open began paying equal prize money to men and women at the 1973 U.S. Open.

Shortly after, King played Bobby Riggs in the *"Battle of the Sexes,"* an event King is best known for today. Over 90 million people from around the world watched as King took on Riggs, who had proclaimed himself a chauvinist, and stated on numerous occasions that the women's tennis game was inferior to the men's.

Bobby was in his 50s at the time, but he was a number one ranked player in the 1930s and 1940s and kept insisting that even at his age he could beat the top women players.

Bobby challenged King to a match and she bravely took him on. On September 20, 1973, King and Riggs played a match in the Houston Astrodome, in the most widely watched tennis match of all time. King beat Riggs in every set, 6-4, 6-3, 6-3, and took home $100,000 in prize money.

"The Battle of the Sexes" did much more than earn King a popular reputation and $100,000 in prize money. The victory, along with the passage of Title IX—a law that protects people from discrimination based on sex in education programs or activities, such as sports, that receive Federal financial assistance—are considered to be the two driving forces behind a huge increase in women's participation in sports.

This also inspired women to fight for equal pay in all fields. By taking on male chauvinist Bobby Riggs, King earned women athletes respect and empowered them to have confidence in their abilities.

After the *"Battle of the Sexes,"* King founded the Women's Sports Foundation, dedicated to developing leaders by giving girls the resources they need to have access to sports. The Women's Sports Foundation is still alive and well today. They sponsor research and provide funds to aspiring women athletes who show promise, as well as advocating on behalf of women athletes around the world. King still serves on the organization's board.

Despite her world-renowned success and obvious talent, King lost all of her endorsements when she was publicly outed as a lesbian. She had started a secret relationship with a woman, Marilyn Barnett, in the 1970s. They had a relationship for seven years that ended in 1979. After ending their relationship, King asked Barnett to leave her Malibu house where she had been allowing her to stay. Barnett decided to sue King publicly for lifetime support and King had to decide how to proceed.

Against the advice of her attorney, who pressed her not to tell the truth, King decided to come out publicly. In 1981, King announced her affair with Barnett during a press conference. King became the first famous female athlete to come out as a lesbian.

In 1981, Barnett attempted suicide after the conclusion of the trial and was paralyzed from the waist down. No comments by King exist on public record regarding the actions of

Barnett. When asked in retrospect if she would have done anything differently, King said, *"I would have come out earlier."*

There was a ton of shame associated with homosexuality in the 1970s and King was not immune to that. Her parents were at the press conference with her in 1981 when she came out and there were reportedly tears in their eyes. King claims she didn't fully feel comfortable with being gay until her mid-50s, after extensive therapy to undo the trauma of society's homophobia.

The affair nearly destroyed King's career, and she could have let it break her: but she didn't. She continued her fight against inequality in all shapes and forms and continued to play tennis. King has long been an inspiration to LGBTQ individuals. She continuously speaks up encouraging the younger generation to help create a more inclusive world.

In 1981, when she was 38 years old, King became the oldest female semifinalist at Wimbledon since 1920. One year later, she became the oldest female player to win a singles tournament at the Birmingham tournament.

King officially retired from competitive tennis in 1984. Throughout her tennis career, King won 129 singles titles and her total prize money totals almost US$2 million. In 1987, she was inducted into the International Tennis Hall of Fame.

She embraced her identity and found love again after her divorce from Larry King in 1987. King lives in New York City with her partner, Ilana Kloss, and the two remain good friends with Larry King.

King became the first woman to have a major sports venue named after her. The USTA National Tennis Center in Flushing, NY was dedicated as the USTA Billie Jean King National Tennis Center on August 28, 2006.

On August 12, 2009, Billie Jean King was awarded the highest civilian honor that one can achieve in the United States: The Presidential Medal of Freedom. President Barack Obama presented her with the award in a ceremony at the White House, in Washington, D.C. She became the first female sports player to ever receive this great honor.

As of 2020, King is still alive and well, fighting for the causes she believes in.

BILLIE JEAN KING: DID YOU KNOW?

1. As a child who grew up in a conservative, Methodist household, King wanted to be a preacher when she grew up.

2. When King was attending Los Angeles State College, she received a harsh lesson in the inequalities that existed for women during that time. Although she was an extremely talented tennis player, she was denied a scholarship because of her gender.

3. In 1972, King became the first woman to ever be chosen as magazine *Sports Illustrated "Sportsperson of the Year."*

4. Elton John wrote his hit song, *"Philadelphia Freedom,"* for King, to commemorate her becoming the first woman to coach a co-ed professional sports team.

5. To celebrate the 35th Anniversary of the *"Battle of the Sexes"* tennis match, King wrote a book, *Pressure is a Privilege: Lessons I've Learned from Life and the Battle of the Sexes.*

6. The film *Battle of the Sexes,* starring award-winning actors Emma Stone and Steve Carell, was released in 2017. The plot follows the infamous match between King and Riggs in 1973. Both Stone and Carell were nominated for Golden Globe awards for their performances in the hit film.

7. In 1990, King was recognized by *LIFE* magazine, who

named her on their *"100 Most Important Americans of the 20th Century"* list. She wasn't included just as a talented tennis player but also for her life's work to promote the rights of women in sports, particularly through the Women's Sports Foundation.

8. After being inspired by tennis player Althea Gibson's book, *I Always Wanted to be Somebody,* King founded the Billie Jean King Leadership Initiative in 2014, to foster a movement where diverse talent is celebrated. Her initiative, a non-profit organization, focuses on addressing the issues our society faces in acquiring diversity and inclusive leadership in the workforce.

9. In 1990, King was inducted into the National Women's Hall of Fame, a non-profit in Seneca Falls, New York, which honors the accomplishments of America's most influential and outstanding women. It's located at the site of the first Women's Rights Convention held in 1848.

10. The Long Beach City Council honored King by naming a Long Beach library after her, designating it as the Billie Jean King Main Library in 2019.

CONCLUSION

Women have never been given their rights; badass women have always had to fight for them. The 15 inspirational, ferocious heroines in this book are responsible for so much, including the right for women to vote, get an education, pursue jobs in fields previously barred to them, and being paid equally in (some) sports competitions, as well as having access to life-saving vaccines.

The women in this book never gave up; they fought for equality, and they defied the stereotypes of their times. They faced fear and didn't falter; the Mirabal sisters literally lost their lives fighting for justness for their country. One of the unique things about many of these women is that they not only worked individually to change the world but in doing so, they inspired others to follow them. As Ruth Bader Ginsburg once said, *"Fight for the things that you care about, but do it in a way that will lead others to join you."*

Although women—especially women of color—have largely been excluded from our history books, these unsung heroes have always been there, kicking ass. By telling their stories, we preserve their legacies and inspire others to follow in their footsteps.

By acknowledging women's history, we also help bust the myths about all the things people still think women cannot do. Many men still don't think women should fight in war, but they've been doing it for centuries.

There probably aren't a lot of men out there who can say that they have single-handedly killed the enemy with their bare hands, using a swift karate-chop to the throat, like the badass resistance fighter, Nancy Wake. Many female nurses are still fighting for respect in the workplace, yet there are millions of Florence Nightingales out there who are on the front lines every day.

Across the globe, women have come a long way, but there is still a long way to go. Paid maternity leave isn't mandatory in the United States, men still earn more money than women for the same work, women in Afghanistan face forced marriage, and women make up 50% of the world's population that lives in poverty.

There is still so much to be done, and badass women like Malala, the Notorious RBG, and Billie Jean King are still fighting to break down barriers every day.

Made in the USA
Coppell, TX
23 November 2022

86944275R00079